ALSO BY GENE STONE
The Bush Survival Bible

DUCK!

DUCK!

The
Dick Cheney
Survival Bible

250 Ways to Find Cover from the Man
Who Calls the Shots, Pulls the Strings,
and Shoots the Lawyers

Gene Stone
with Carl Pritzkat and Tony Travostino

VILLARD **V** NEW YORK

A Villard Books Trade Paperback Original

Copyright © 2006 by Gene Stone

Published in the United States by Villard Books, an imprint of The Random House Publishing Group, a division of Random House, Inc., New York.

VILLARD and "V" CIRCLED Design are registered trademarks of Random House, Inc.

Photos from "5 Bad Dogs Speak Out on Cheney" used with the permission of Workman Publishing Co., Inc., New York City, publishers of *Bad Dog*. © 2006 by R. D. Rosen, Harry Prichett, and Rob Battles, photographs copyright © by Workman Publishing Co., Inc. BAD DOG is a trademark of Workman Publishing

ISBN 0-8129-7729-7

Printed in the United States of America

www.villard.com

987654321

This book is dedicated to everyone who ever had a nightmare and couldn't wake up.

Contents

INTRODUCTION xiii

6 Vice-Presidential Duties 3

**4 Characterizations of the Vice Presidency,
by Vice Presidents** 6

**12 Important Moments in
Vice-Presidential History** 7

**6 Ways to Test Your "Could I Be Dick Cheney's
Best Friend?" Affinity** 12
by Bruce McCall

6 Archetypal Dick Cheney Quotes 15

**6 Rules That Will Keep You from Getting
Shot While Hunting with Vice President
Dick Cheney** 16
by Lucian K. Truscott IV

**8 Historical Figures Shot
in Hunting Accidents** 19

4 Steps to Take If You're Shot in the Face 23
by Mark Liponis

11 Books in Dick Cheney's Library 26

8 Dick Cheney Conspiracy Theories 27

5 Political Oilmen and Oily Politicians 31

**5 Ways to Decorate Your
Undisclosed Location** 36

**10 Most Destructive Lies
Dick Cheney Has Told** 40

5 Strangest Lies Dick Cheney Has Told 44

9 Lies Dick Cheney Hasn't Told . . . 46

10 Ways to Tell If You're Dick Cheney 48

7 Movies to See with Dick Cheney 51

**5 Vice Presidents Worse Than
Dick Cheney** 52
by Joshua Hammer

**7 Groups You Can Join to Fight
Dick Cheney** 56

5 Bad Dogs Speak Out on Cheney 61
by R. D. Rosen, Harry Prichett, and Rob Battles

**7 People Who Hate Dick Cheney
More Than You Do** 67

9 Other Famous Dicks 73

**4 Ways to Recover from a Bad Speech
Even If You've Just Shot a Man
or Launched a War** 79
by Francis Wilkinson

5 Things to Expect Dick Cheney to Do as Global Warming Intensifies 83
by *Eugene Linden*

8 Ways Dick Cheney Secretly Controls Intelligence 87

7 Haiku as Written by Dick Cheney 91

6 Ideas for Campaign Reform 93
by *Doris "Granny D" Haddock*

7 Steps to Creating Your Dick Cheney Protest Record 96
by *John Hartmann*

8 of Dick Cheney's Favorite Foods 101

8 Reasons Why Not All Oilfield Workers Support Dick Cheney 102
by *George Lattimore*

5 Editorial Cartoons About Dick Cheney 106

5 Flawed Vice Presidents 109

5 Ways to Stay Alive If You Suspect Your Date Is a Dick Cheney Sympathizer 117
by *Laurie Notaro*

8 Steps to Take If You Believe the Government Is Spying on You 120
by *X*

12 Places to Go Online 123

9 Songs on Dick Cheney's iPod 127

**4 Ways to Tell If Your Husband Is
Turning into Dick Cheney—and
What to Do About It** 128
by Terry Real

4 Steps to Impeachment 130

1 Last Thing to Worry About 135

Acknowledgments 137

Introduction

Why, you may wonder, a book on surviving Dick Cheney? He's not going to shoot you. Or at least, the odds aren't that high. You're probably not rich or powerful enough to be invited on one of his hunting trips. And besides, he's a bad shot.

Well, once you think about it, there actually are plenty of bad things Dick Cheney could do to you. He could start a war on a false pretext and send your friends and children off to fight in it. He could drive oil prices up so high that you will no longer be able to commute. He could raise your debt to a preposterously high level (while telling you that "deficits don't matter"). He could tap your phone without your knowledge and post your conversations on a local bulletin board. He could hire thugs to torture your family—no explanation required.

When people truly grasp the concept of Dick Cheney, they become scared. *Really* scared. "I had a nightmare the other night," they remember, "and it was about the vice president!" Or they realize, "When my toddler saw him on TV, she burst into tears and ran from the room!" Or they recall, "That's the man whose face broke my mirrors and whose voice made the dog howl."

Dick Cheney isn't just the vice president of the United

States anymore. He is something much larger and more intimidating. Dick Cheney is the scariest man in America.

You can see and hear the signs all across the country. Parents warn their children that if they don't eat their broccoli, Dick Cheney will get them. Teachers tell students that if they skip classes, the principal will sic Dick Cheney on them. Girl Scouts sit around campfires, shocking each other with hideous yarns about Dick Cheney.

As the months pass, the Dick Cheney legend only grows. Hollywood has been flooded with high-concept Dick Cheney scripts: Innocent people turning into him when bitten by young Republicans. Dick takes on Damien, spawn of the Antichrist. *Jason versus Freddy versus Dick. Alien versus Predator versus the Vice President. Bride of Cheney. Son of Cheney. Darth Cheney. Dick Cheney Takes Over the Whole Goddamn World, Enslaves the Human Race, and Marries Satan.*

Meanwhile, historians have uncovered pictures of Dick Cheney on the *Titanic.* His photo was found in Lizzie Borden's purse and in Jack the Ripper's backpack. Anthropologists have discovered his likeness on totem polls, and archeologists have unearthed his image in ancient ruins.

The bottom line in America today: You don't have to be a Democrat to fear Dick Cheney. Polls show his approval rating hovers below Michael Jackson's numbers during his trial for alleged child molestation, or O. J. Simpson's while he was on trial for killing his wife. People are afraid. Very afraid.

So the next time the full moon rises and vampire bats fly shrieking from their caves, don't take to the hills. Take out a copy of *Duck!* for cover. Besides giving you advice, consolation, and companionship, it's less smelly than garlic, cheaper than a silver bullet, and doesn't need to be blessed by a priest.

Gene Stone and the *Dick Cheney Survival Bible* Squad:
> Polly King
> Carl Pritzkat
> Miranda Spencer
> Tony Travostino
> Jen White

March 2006

Please visit our website: TheDickCheneySurvivalBible.com

DUCK!

6 Vice-Presidential Duties

In his book *Vice Presidents of the United States, 1789–1993*, former senator Mark Hatfield called the office of the vice presidency "the least understood, most ridiculed, and most often ignored constitutional office in the federal government."

Here are some reasons why; this is what the veep actually does.

1. The vice president holds office for the same duration as the president (four years) and must meet the same criteria as the commander in chief. Namely: Be at least thirty-five years old, a natural-born U.S. citizen, and a resident of the United States for at least fourteen years. The rationale: He (or she) can become president at any minute.

2. The vice president serves as the number two official in the executive branch of United States government and is first in line of succession. This means he takes over the job if the president dies (Lincoln), resigns

(Nixon), or is removed from office (Clinton—almost). Ditto if the president is temporarily unable to do his job (as when Ronald Reagan underwent colon surgery).

3. The vice president is the president of the U.S. Senate. This mostly ceremonial job has two main components:

   a. Overseeing procedural matters. Early veeps such as John Adams and Thomas Jefferson took a heavy hand in running the Senate's day-to-day affairs, and their decisions were set in stone. Later veeps have been actively involved or lackadaisical, depending on their personalities and preferences. In the twentieth century, they've usually had their hands full with other concerns (such as heading energy task forces). Thus the Senate is usually run by a president pro tempore, selected by its members.

   b. Voting to break a stalemate. This role kicks in when all one hundred Senate members vote and are split fifty-fifty. It's the only time the vice president gets to vote.

      This seldom happens; tiebreaking votes have been needed only 233 times in the country's history. Then again, Dick Cheney is among the top ten vice presidents with the greatest number of tiebreaking votes (seven). The privilege came in handy early in the Bush II administration, when the Senate was evenly divided along party lines; Dick Cheney gave the Republicans a fifty-one to fifty majority.

4. In the presence of Congress, the standing vice president is the one who opens and counts all electoral votes for the offices of president and vice president in a national election.

5. The vice president is authorized to nominate individuals to the United States Military, Naval, and Air Force academies (but not the Coast Guard or Merchant Marine academies).

   If you or your child wants to attend West Point, you must write to the vice president personally.

6. The vice president handles unofficial jobs. Most of the time, the vice president does whatever the president finds for him or allows him to do. Some of the assignments essayed by modern veeps include the following:

   • Attend cabinet meetings
   • Serve on the National Security Council
   • Head or participate on commissions and task forces
   • Advise the president on matters of policy according to their own expertise
   • Represent the U.S. government to foreign heads of state
   • Help balance the ticket at election time, and provide a successor for a two-term president that keeps the prevailing party in power

As envisioned by the framers of the Constitution, the vice president is not supposed to exploit his position by lobbying or strong-arming Congress or otherwise acting partisan. Of course, that concept is so 1776.

4 Characterizations of the Vice Presidency, by Vice Presidents

1. "The most insignificant office that ever the invention of man contrived or his imagination conceived."

    —*John Adams, vice president to George Washington*

2. "Not worth a pitcher of warm piss."

    —*John Nance Garner, vice president to*
    Franklin Delano Roosevelt

3. "The President has only 190 million bosses. The Vice President has 190 million and one."

    —*Hubert H. Humphrey, vice president to Lyndon Johnson*

4. "One word sums up probably the responsibility of any vice president, and that one word is 'to be prepared.' "

    —*Dan Quayle, vice president to George Bush*

12 Important Moments in Vice-Presidential History

Since the veep's job has always been somewhat ambiguous, and not particularly powerful, vice-presidential history tends to revolve around events connected to the office itself, such as how people attained it, as well as how they left it.

1. Presidential Succession Act, 1792

     What if the president dies and there's no veep to take his place? No one knew. That's why this law came into effect, specifying that the Senate president pro tem gets the job, and if for some reason he can't, the Speaker of the House is up next.

2. Twelfth Amendment to the Constitution, 1804

     Up until this point, the vice president was the person who came in second in the presidential election (in the number of electoral votes, and assuming some candidate won a majority). If there was a tie, the House of Representatives would vote to resolve it. This could have awkward results, as when the president and vice president came from two different parties. (Imagine a John McCain–Hillary Clinton White House.)

When Thomas Jefferson and Aaron Burr tied for president in 1800, the House cast ballots thirty-five times before a winner could be called. That led to the situation we have now, where the president and his selection for vice president run as a team, and electors vote for them on separate ballots.

3. First Vice-Presidential Shooting, 1804

Vice President Aaron Burr fatally wounded longtime rival, former Treasury secretary Alexander Hamilton, in a duel at Weehawken, New Jersey, over an alleged insult. Burr fired first, and killed Hamilton, who, most scholars say, shot his gun in the air to avoid bloodshed.

4. First Vice-Presidential Resignation, 1832

Andrew Jackson's vice president, John C. Calhoun, who had many political and personal battles both with the senators over whom he presided and with Jackson himself, resigned from office when he was elected to become a senator, proving, if anyone needed to know, that most people would rather be a senator than a veep.

5. Tyler's Takeover, 1841

Article II, Section I, of the Constitution says if the president dies or can't do his job, the "Powers and Duties of the said Office . . . shall devolve on the Vice President." Did that mean temporarily or permanently? No one was sure.

When William Henry Harrison died in office, Vice President John Tyler set the precedent, deciding that the clause meant he'd assume both the job and the perks of the chief exec. Congress and the American people let Tyler's decision stand.

6. VP Succession Tackled Again, 1886

Congress decided it would be better if members of the late president's cabinet were next in line if for some reason there was no vice president, starting with the secretary of state. (Leading to Secretary of State Al Haig's 1981 assertion that "I'm in charge here" when Ronald Reagan was shot. He wasn't.)

7. Presidents Pick Own Running Mates, 1930s to present

For more than a century, party honchos tended to select the candidate for vice president, regardless of whether he got along with the candidate running for president—and sometimes, in fact, when the two disliked each other. For better or worse, as the government's, and the veep's, role grew following Franklin Roosevelt's New Deal, presidential candidates started choosing their campaign partners.

8. Vice-Presidential Succession Changes Yet Again, 1947

Congress now decided the Speaker of the House should become president if the president died while the vice presidency was vacant. And so it remains today.

9. First Temporary President, 1953 to 1961

As vice president to Dwight D. Eisenhower, Richard M. Nixon was asked to run cabinet meetings and was the first to step in as temporary president (which he did three times) when Ike was out sick from the job. Nixon is also credited with being the first veep to use his office as a direct path to winning the White House.

10. Twenty-fifth Amendment Passed, 1967

After John Kennedy was assassinated in 1963 and Vice President Lyndon B. Johnson took over as presi-

The devil visited Dick Cheney's office with an offer. "If you want to make a deal, I can do anything you want me to do," he said. "I can make you the president for life. I can make Halliburton the richest company on earth. I can guarantee that you will live to be one hundred and fifty and be healthy the entire time. I can give you anything you want.

"All I ask in return is for your wife's soul, your children's souls, and your grandchildren's souls to rot in hell for all of eternity."

Dick thought it over carefully. Then he asked, "But what's the catch?"

"But all kidding aside, and in fairness to Dick Cheney, every five years he has to shed innocent blood or he violates his deal with the devil."

—Jimmy Kimmel

"He is a lawyer and he got shot in the face. But he's a lawyer, he can use his other face. He'll be all right."

—Craig Ferguson

dent, Congress decided to clarify vice-presidential succession once and for all by amending the Constitution. The amendment states that the president gets to appoint a new vice president when the office becomes vacant, as long as both houses of Congress approve.

The amendment also spells out, in tedious detail, exactly when and how the veep is permitted to serve temporarily as "Acting President."

11. Second Vice-Presidential Resignation, 1968 to 1973

Spiro T. Agnew, Richard M. Nixon's vice president, had been promised an actual role in policymaking and was the first veep to be bestowed an office in the West Wing. He was also the most blatant in his efforts to actively lobby the Senate on legislation. Agnew eventually pleaded no contest to tax evasion, paid a fine, and resigned.

12. Second Vice-Presidential Shooting, 2006

Vice President Dick Cheney shot his friend Harry Whittington in the face during a quail-hunting trip in Texas. News of the incident did not reach the press for almost a day. While in the hospital recuperating, Whittington suffered a heart attack; upon his discharge, he apologized to the vice president, who faced no legal charges but whose approval rating fell to 18 percent.

6 Ways to Test Your "Could I Be Dick Cheney's Best Friend?" Affinity

Bruce McCall

Bruce McCall is a New York writer and artist whose satire appears regularly in The New Yorker, Vanity Fair, *and other magazines. He is currently working on his first children's book.*

Official disclosure: Your chances of becoming Dick Cheney's friend are approximately one in 231 million. Devious, disingenuous, and dishonest answers will not be accepted.

1. Check the belief that best matches Dick's:
   a. I don't need friends _____
   b. Friends are people you haven't screwed yet _____
   c. Friends don't whine when you plug them _____
       Correct Answer: Dick Cheney's personal friendship philosophy is a secret covered by the Patriot Act, Executive Privilege, and the Healthy Forests Initiative. Back off if you know what's good for you.
2. While visiting a friend in the hospital, Dick:
   a. eats their lunch _____

   b. throws their lunch at the TV, which is not tuned to
Fox _____

   c. changes his mind in the parking lot and flies to
Wyoming for a beef 'n' bourbon church social
instead _____

     Correct Answer: None of the above. Dick Cheney
has no friends in hospitals. They all, including Dick,
choose only fat-cat private clinics.

3. Dick Cheney is old and fat with a bum ticker but
does not fear death because:

   a. God wouldn't dare _____

   b. he has connections in heaven that will set him up
there with even more special perks than he has
here on earth _____

   c. his doctors know what will happen to them if he
croaks _____

     Correct Answer: (a). Being denied access to Dick's
personal medical records, God wouldn't know if he
were to croak.

4. Dick Cheney keeps signed photos of which close pals
in his den?

   a. Idi Amin _____

   b. Emperor Bokassa _____

   c. Papa Doc _____

   d. Baby Doc _____

   e. Gadhafi _____

   f. Saudi royal family (group picture) _____

     Correct Answer: All of the above plus six other
Saudi royal family group pictures.

5. Dick Cheney evaded the draft and avoided serving
his country in the military during the Vietnam War
because:

   a. his battlefield heroism would have overshadowed

that of thousands of others and created morale problems _____

b. his dog ate his draft notice _____

c. he was swimming to the induction center when John Kerry's swift boat came along and "accidentally" knocked him unconscious for the next ten years _____

   Correct Answer: Classified.

6. Dick Cheney asks you to deliver $1 million in cash to Jack Abramoff, but while carrying out his request, you are apprehended by the cops. You:

a. commit hara-kiri _____

b. finger Senator Feingold (D-Wisconsin) _____

c. claim you were en route to a secret meeting on the administration's energy policy and are immune to even being asked questions _____

   Correct Answer: Who are you? Dick Cheney doesn't know anybody by that name. It must be a mix-up. Stop calling.

6 Archetypal Dick Cheney Quotes

1. "Except for the occasional heart attack, I never felt better."

   —*June 4, 2003*

2. "I had other priorities in the sixties than military service."

   —*on his five draft deferments, April 5, 1989*

3. "Conservation may be a sign of personal virtue but it is not a sufficient basis for a sound, comprehensive energy policy."

   —*April 30, 2001*

4. "My belief is we will, in fact, be greeted as liberators."

   —*March 16, 2003*

5. "Simply stated, there is no doubt that Saddam now has weapons of mass destruction."

   —*August 8, 2002*

6. "Go f**k yourself."

   —*to Senator Patrick Leahy, during an angry exchange on the Senate floor about profiteering by Halliburton, June 25, 2004*

6 Rules That Will Keep You from Getting Shot While Hunting with Vice President Dick Cheney

Lucian K. Truscott IV

Lucian K. Truscott IV was born into one of America's most distinguished military families, and himself entered West Point but ran into a dispute with the army over an article he wrote for the Village Voice *about the rampant problem of heroin abuse in the army. What the army used to call "a flap" ensued, and Truscott's resignation from the army followed. He then worked for the* Village Voice *before becoming a freelance writer, contributing to such magazines as* The New York Times Magazine, The New Yorker, Esquire, The Nation, Harper's, *and* Rolling Stone. *He also wrote the bestselling novel* Dress Gray *in 1979, which was later produced as an NBC miniseries, scripted by Gore Vidal. Truscott also wrote the bestsellers* Army Blue, Heart of War, *and* Full Dress Gray, *as well as many screenplays. He lives in Los Angeles with his wife and his two children.*

Hunting wild game is an ancient and honorable practice with roots in the lifestyles of the rich and Paleolithic, who ventured forth on foot into the hills and dales in order to procure, in a primitive sense, Meat for the Table. Since that time, hunting has devolved in almost every way from its ancient and honorable traditions. Gone is "wild" from wild game, replaced by well-trained birds or fur-bearing mammals who have been hired to make themselves easily available to golfers with big guns who might otherwise fail to procure untrained targets bent on indulging a tendency to fly off or run in any and all directions at once.

Gone is "foot" from venturing forth on foot, replaced by traveling uphill and down dale via such modes of transportation as straddling a $9,800.00 Tony Stewart Signature Mongo Four Wheeler, or swaddling oneself with Corinthian leather in an old Land Cruiser or International Scout that has undergone a $50,000 frame-up restoration, complete with Dual Auto Dash-Mounted Martini Shakers.

Gone, too, is the whole idea of procuring meat for the table by golfers with big guns who brag that they have killed in excess of ninety quail on a single "shoot" and have no intention whatsoever of sitting down and gnawing on that many teeny-tiny-itty-bitty-eensey-weensey little drumsticks.

Present is the need to keep oneself free of a face and upper body scarred by half a load of number $7\frac{1}{2}$ birdshot as expelled by the vice president. Here are the Rules that I, as a Gun Safety Expert, have outlined for you, so pay close attention.

1. Dick Cheney skipped Vietnam, but he's fighting his war right now out there on the Battlefield of the Bobtailed Quail. It's a war of attrition, so it will help to read General Giap, Sun Tzu, von Clausewitz, and Chairman Mao. They know things Dick Cheney and his pals don't know, as evidenced by the so-called war in Iraq. Their tactics will serve you well on the hunt.

2. Don't go hunting with guys whose shotguns cost more than your house.

3. A man can't hit what he can't see. Don't wear an International Orange hunting vest. Dress yourself head to toe in camouflage befitting the surrounding terrain. Blend in. Stay out of sight. Better still, stay out of their line of sight.

4. Brush up on the Infantry Tactics manual chapter on the Low Crawl, a belly-to-the-ground, earth-hugging maneuver that is the only appropriate way to approach a firing line occupied by Dick Cheney and other golfers carrying big guns.

5. If the presence of fire ants or contaminated soil necessitates standing up during one's approach to a firing line of Republican BarcaLounger Battalioneers, hold a large Kevlar-reinforced satchel filled with packets of large-denomination American money as a shield in front of your upper torso and neck. You could fashion an adequate Kevlar satchel by stitching together a double thickness of combat vests cast off by soldiers who raised enough money from friends and family to buy more effective vests on the open market. Make certain you overlap the below-standard Kevlar "plates" in the military-issue vests, or you may end up being marked for life as the prey of a very angry man who was reduced to shooting a load of birdshot instead of his wad.

6. Don't go hunting with golfers carrying big guns who know the sheriff.

8 Historical Figures Shot in Hunting Accidents

1. William II of England

    August 2, 1100. King William Rufus (William II) was hunting in the forest with his younger brother Henry, Walter Tirel, and two other brothers, Robert de Clare and Gilbert de Clare. At some point Walter Tirel shot his arrow at a deer and hit the king, who died shortly thereafter; Mr. Tirel fled on his horse to France.

    Some historians have suggested that the shooting was a plot between the de Clares and Henry to give the latter the throne. William Rufus was the younger son of William the Conqueror. His elder brother, Robert, had wanted to rule Normandy, but his father didn't agree, and Robert took up arms against his father. William Rufus stuck with his father the king, and was later given the crown, thus bypassing Robert.

    When William Rufus died, Henry, worrying that his eldest brother Robert would now claim the throne, rushed back to gain control of the treasury and claimed the kingdom, with the support of the de Clares. Robert made idle threats, but recognition and allegiance to his brother was bought with an annual stipend.

2. Photisarath

Photisarath was a devout sixteenth-century Buddhist king who razed the shrines of animism and witchcraft and built temples in their place throughout Laos. It's debatable whether this gained him any good karma: The story goes that, while hunting with his entourage in an attempt to impress them with his skills, he was crushed by his elephant when it fell on him.

3. Antônio de Castro Alves

A well-known Brazilian poet born in the mid-nineteenth century, Castro Alves was famous for his opposition to slavery. Castro Alves, the son of a doctor, went to law school, where he first started composing poetry. While hunting near São Paolo, he was shot in his left ankle, which eventually had to be amputated. He dropped out of law school, and dedicated himself to a wild bohemian lifestyle and his writing. He died of tuberculosis at the age of twenty-four.

4. Lambert of Spoleto

King of Italy (such as it was in the late 800s), Lambert held the country jointly with his father until the latter's death, when Lambert became sole king and emperor. However, the land was not calm, and the king was besieged by rivals trying to usurp the throne; three years after his coronation, Lambert was deposed by proxy and another king was crowned.

However, when that king died, Lambert returned to the throne, ordering the dead body of the ex-king to be put on trial, convicted, stripped, mutilated, and thrown into the Tiber River.

Somehow, Lambert still had enemies, and after going on a hunting trip south of Milan, he was either accidentally or purposefully killed. Sometimes it's hard to tell an accident from murder, especially when it happened over a thousand years ago.

5. King Philip the Fair

Although he was called the Fair, Philip was not much of a gentleman, and once had all of the Knights Templars executed on false charges. The knights proclaimed their innocence and, before being put to death, their leader cursed Philip, saying that he would not live to the end of the year and, incidentally, that the pope would die within forty days. The pope didn't last even that long, and later that same year (1314), Philip died in a hunting accident.

6. Louis IV, Holy Roman Emperor

When Louis IV was declared emperor in the fourteenth century, the pope objected, maintaining that the imperial throne was still vacant, as the pope had not affirmed the declaration. Later, when Louis traveled to Rome, his ascension was ratified by the representatives of the Roman people and eventually, after much discussion in Latin, a decree was made that the papacy wasn't needed when it came to naming the emperor.

During his rule, Louis often deeded out large parcels of land to his relatives. For instance, he gave Holland to his wife. Taking advantage of the growing discontent with Louis, the pope named a new emperor, and while Louis was successful in resisting the new church-ordained upstart, he was conveniently killed in a hunting accident in 1347.

7. The husband of Saint Jane Frances de Chantal

At twenty, she married the Baron de Chantal, an officer in Henry IV's army, and then turned his family fortunes around. But eight years into the marriage, the baron went hunting with a friend who, seeing a dark figure moving in the growth, lifted his harquebus to his shoulder, took aim at the wild beast, and shot. Unfortunately, the wild beast was the baron, suddenly deceased.

Widowed at twenty-eight, Saint Jane Frances went to live with her wicked father-in-law, spending her time in prayer until she received a vision of the man who would become her spiritual mentor. She eventually met that man and founded the Order of the Visitation of Our Lady. Saint Jane Frances's reputation for sanctity was extensive, and royalty often came to visit. She was beatified in 1751 and canonized in 1767, and August 21 was appointed as her feast day. Today she is patroness to forgotten people, widows, those with in-law problems, and, possibly, people shot by vice presidents.

8. Greg LeMond

In 1986 LeMond was the first American bicyclist to win the Tour de France. Soon after that he was shot by his brother-in-law while hunting. He took approximately fifty shotgun pellets in his back, side, and legs. Shot also lodged internally in his diaphragm, intestine, liver, and heart lining. Had it not been for the helicopter that airlifted him to the hospital, he would have died. Three years later, he won the Tour de France again.

4 Steps to Take If You're Shot in the Face

Mark Liponis

Mark Liponis, M.D., is the corporate medical director of Canyon Ranch, the world's leading health resort, and the co-author of the bestselling book Ultraprevention *(Scribner, 2002). His newest book,* Ultra-Immunity, *will be published by Little, Brown in 2007.*

Getting shot in the face by a round of lead buckshot is a serious occurrence, and one that needs immediate attention. On the other hand, getting shot in the face by the vice president of the United States could be considered a good-news, bad-news proposition.

The bad news is that if you're on Medicare, your insurance will cover only a fraction of the cost of your medical care.

The good news is that you will be receiving a prescription voucher for OxyContin on the new White House Medicare prescription plan.

The bad news is you could be killed or permanently disfigured.

The good news is that you could now become eligible

for Social Security disability before cuts and insolvency eliminate benefits altogether.

The bad news is it really hurts.

The good news is it hurts him a heck of a lot more.

The bad news is you could get lead poisoning.

The good news is that it would have been much worse if you were a quail.

Here's what you need to know and what to do if you're shot by buckshot:

1. With acute serious injuries, the very first steps are the ABCs: airway, breathing, and circulation.
   a. Maintain an open airway by proper positioning of the head and neck, or by thrusting the jaw forward manually and gently lifting the jaw.
   b. If necessary, support breathing with mouth-to-mouth resuscitation.
   c. Elevate and apply direct pressure to active bleeding sites.
2. Next, call 911 to activate the emergency medical system for transport to the nearest trauma center.
3. Beware of delayed complications such as infection, blood clots, and heart attacks. Embedded low-velocity buckshot carries a higher risk of infection than high-velocity bullets (which are rendered sterile by the heat of the explosion and their velocity). Signs of infection include fever, redness, swelling, and pain.
4. It may surprise you that buckshot will likely stay inside the body indefinitely and should not necessarily be surgically removed. Rarely, delayed migration of these pellets into the bloodstream and brain, causing stroke, has been reported.

A doctor had just settled into his new villa on the French Riviera, where he encountered his old friend Dick Cheney, whom he hadn't seen in many years. The two men talked about the major events in their lives and how they both came to retire on the Riviera.

"Do you remember all those bad oil wells I bought in the West?" Dick Cheney asked the doctor. "Well, they all caught fire, and I retired here with the fire insurance proceeds. What are you doing here?"

The doctor replied, "Remember that real estate I had in Mississippi? Well, after the hurricane, the river overflowed, and here I am with the flood insurance proceeds. It's amazing that we both ended up here in pretty much the same way."

"It sure is," Dick Cheney said, but he looked puzzled, so the doctor asked him what was on his mind.

"Well, I'm really confused about one thing," Dick Cheney said. "How do you start a hurricane?"

"Homeland Security director Tom Ridge has unveiled a new color-coded system to warn the public about different states of danger. Red is the highest state of alert, and it means that Dick Cheney is about to eat a mozzarella stick."

—Conan O'Brien

"You can't blame [Cheney]. Bush says you can spy on people without warrants, you can torture people, you can hold people without a trial, so Dick Cheney thinks, 'Oh what the hell, I can shoot a few guys.'"

—Jay Leno

11 Books in Dick Cheney's Library

1. *A Farewell to Arms Inspectors*
2. *My Heart of Darkness*
3. *Oil Wells That End Well*
4. *To Kill a Penned-Up-Clipped-Winged-Game-Hunting Bird*
5. *The Once and Future King George*
6. *I Know Why the Caged Iraqi Sings*
7. *No Remembrance of Things Past*
8. *The Artificial Heart Is a Lonely Hunter*
9. *One Hundred Years of Prisoners in Solitude*
10. *The Joy of Cooking Intelligence*
11. *Eats, Shoots, and Leaves*

8 Dick Cheney Conspiracy Theories

1. Plotting the November Massacre

   In 1975, while working with President Gerald Ford's chief of staff, Donald Rumsfeld, Dick Cheney plotted with the future secretary of defense to push out cabinet members, most notably Henry Kissinger, who were politically moderate and open to détente with the Soviet Union. The resulting shake-up, known as the Halloween Massacre, landed Dick Cheney the job of chief of staff and Rumsfeld that of secretary of defense, forced Kissinger out as head of the National Security Council, and replaced the CIA director with a new face, George H. W. Bush. All this weakened moderate Vice President Nelson Rockefeller's influence on the president and helped provoke his formal withdrawal as Ford's running mate in the 1976 election.

2. Undermining the Iran-Contra Hearings

   A decade later Dick Cheney was a conservative Republican in Congress, where, as ranking Republican on the House Intelligence committee and its

Iran-Contra hearings, he aggressively fought to block any attempts by Democrats to get information from the Reagan White House. Dick Cheney also went out of his way to prevent then vice president George H. W. Bush, largely thought to be one of the masterminds behind the operations, from being called to testify. When Bush became president, he pardoned many of the Iran-Contra operatives, including Elliott Abrams and Robert McFarlane, who returned to work for the Dick Cheney team in the second Bush administration.

3. End-running the Joint Chiefs

As secretary of defense in the first Bush administration, Dick Cheney called on crony Paul Wolfowitz to develop a plan for dispatching Iraq's Saddam Hussein that was much more hawkish than those developed by General Colin Powell, then chairman of the Joint Chiefs of Staff. Dick Cheney kept the proposal, code-named Operation Scorpion, secret from Powell; he then waited until Powell was overseas and presented it to the president. Bush rejected the plan, as he did Dick Cheney's later suggestion the president declare war without congressional approval. The U.S. general in charge of allied forces in the Gulf War, Norman Schwarzkopf, learned of the vice president's backhandedness and was enraged. "Put a civilian in charge of professional military men and before long he's no longer satisfied with setting policy but wants to outgeneral the generals," Schwarzkopf wrote in his memoir.

4. Devising Halliburton's Slippery Operations

One of Dick Cheney's principal acts as secretary of defense was to establish the concept of outsourcing military logistics, and the company to which he gave a hefty share of this new business was Halliburton. Jobless after Bill Clinton's arrival in the White House, Dick Cheney was rewarded by Halliburton with the job of CEO. During his time there, Halliburton's interests thrived in countries with which many other U.S. companies had ceased doing business because of heavy regulation; Cheney used his influence to lobby the U.S. government to relax such regulations.

5. Naming Himself Vice President

When Dick Cheney was asked to help select George W. Bush's vice president, after gathering intelligence on all the other candidates, he named himself. No one knows the inside scoop on how he managed this.

6. Hiding Energy Plans

Back in the White House, now as vice president, one of Dick Cheney's first actions was to convene an energy task force with the goal of redefining the nation's energy policies. The veep stacked the task force with energy industry representatives, including such deep thinkers as Kenneth Lay, CEO of Enron. Industry recommendations were incorporated verbatim into the new policies, and not a single consumer, environmental, or Democratic group was asked to participate.

Highlights from the task force's recommendations included restoring nuclear power as a preferred energy source, relaxing environmental and worker-safety laws to encourage more use of coal, and opening up the Arctic National Wildlife Refuge for oil drilling. But the task force's most notorious deed (and this was months before September 11, 2001) was to examine the energy opportunities that would be offered if the United States were to invade and secure Iraq. Dick Cheney has fiercely and successfully defended all the way to the Supreme Court his right to hide from public review any information about the task force's work.

7. Connecting with Halliburton

Despite repeated claims that he has no financial interest in Halliburton, tax returns and freedom-of-information research show Dick Cheney still receives deferred compensation from the company of $150,000 annually and has stock options valued at more than $18 million. Halliburton has made multiple billions of dollars on no-bid contracts overseen by the vice president's office since the beginning of the war. Indeed, the vice president's office felt so sure Halliburton would get those no-bid contracts that, in 2002, it engaged the company to draw up post-invasion plans before Congress was approached about the invasion.

8. Hunting Accident Cover-up

On February 11, 2006, Dick Cheney shot his hunting companion, seventy-eight-year-old lawyer Harry Whittington, in the face. The vice president's staff kept it from the public—and White House staff—for eighteen hours. Websites and blogs have buzzed about possible reasons for the delay; the main reason for the cover-up, say conspiracy theorists, is that Dick Cheney was drunk.

5 Political Oilmen and Oily Politicians

Like oil and vinegar, oil and politics are a traditional concoction, except that instead of creating salad dressing, they create power. So even if the relationship between Dick Cheney and his on-again, off-again employer, oil giant Halliburton, has raised eyebrows, the vice president is not the first person to combine politics with oil and he won't be the last.

1. John D. Rockefeller (1839–1937)

This former Cleveland accountant founded Standard Oil in 1870 and proceeded to capture a post–Civil War monopoly in oil, eventually becoming America's first billionaire. His strategy: buying up not just refineries, but related industries such as pipelines, shipping tankers, processing factories, and retail stores, and maximizing profits through price fixing, kickback schemes, and secrecy. When money didn't work, Rockefeller used force. Once he got a rancher to sell him land by buying adjacent property, ringing it in barbed wire, and posting armed guards to prevent the man from leaving. In 1873, "the Standard" concentrated production in three huge refineries and came to control 95 percent of America's oil-refining capacity.

In 1882, Rockefeller created the Standard Oil Trust to oversee his empire's holdings. When an Ohio court dissolved the Trust, he reincorporated it in New Jersey. In 1890, when Congress passed the Sherman Antitrust Act to outlaw his iron grip on the market, he simply reincorporated. Finally, in 1892, the Supreme Court dissolved the firm, and J.D. suffered a nervous breakdown.

Note: Rockefeller's grandson, Republican Nelson Rockefeller (1908–1979), was the family man who parlayed his heritage into politics, working for Presidents Roosevelt, Truman, and Eisenhower as well as serving as governor of New York and vice president under Gerald Ford.

2. Andrew W. Mellon (1855–1937)

The son of a Pittsburgh banker, Mellon was one of the richest and most powerful men in the world during the 1920s, thanks to jumbo investments in commodities such as aluminum, steel, and oil. In 1901, his bank financed drilling that yielded an unprecedented amount of black gold near Beaumont, Texas, and he agreed to provide further loans only in exchange for a large chunk of stock; Mellon eventually bought the business and redubbed it Gulf Oil.

Appropriately enough, Mellon served as secretary of the Treasury under Presidents Harding, Coolidge, and Hoover, advocating cuts in government spending and corporate taxes. He got the job as thanks for plugging a $1.5 million deficit in the Republican Party's campaign coffers. In 1926, after Congress passed fiscal legislation recommended by Mellon, the stock market boomed, leading him to a failed 1928 presidential run. After the stock market crash a year later, Mellon was partially blamed due to his promotion of unfettered capitalism; he was nearly impeached, and finally resigned to become ambassador to Britain.

3. Haroldson Lafayette Hunt (1889–1974)

A banker's son from rural Illinois, Hunt began his career as a cardsharp, opening a gambling hall in 1921 during an oil boom in Arkansas, where he started buying leases and drilling. Hunt kept a string of informers to tip him off to oil-rich territory, in which he'd then proceed to invest. When the Depression sank demand for oil, the anti-big-government Hunt supported federal price supports and drilling quotas. In 1936 he incorporated Hunt Oil Company to drill, move, and refine oil; his fortune that year was $20 million. Hunt Oil expanded into other states and sold oil to Germany and Japan before World War II began, and to the U.S. military after.

Hunt also owned a chain of service stations, made a lucrative sideline of gambling, and, by 1948, was called the richest man in America. Hunt's political claim to fame came as a supporter of the Communist-hunting senator Joseph McCarthy. In the 1950s he founded a right-wing political newsletter and radio talk show called *Facts Forum,* staffed with McCarthy's former aides. He later entered Christian fundamentalist broadcasting. (One show railed against President Kennedy the very day he was assassinated.)

4. J. Paul Getty (1892–1976)

Jean Paul Getty was the son of a lawyer–turned–Oklahoma oil wildcatter and later California oil-company millionaire. He entered the oil business in 1914 and was himself a millionaire by age twenty-three through his purchase of low-cost oil leases that rendered giant profits from drilling. Getty took over the family firm, Minnehoma, in 1930. Like Hunt, he exploited the Depression by buying chunks of cheap oil stocks and profiting when the economy rebounded. Getty captured control of his company by convincing the majority shareholder (his mother) to cede control of her trust fund.

A British newspaper recently revealed that Getty not only knew and admired Adolf Hitler, but for a time was supplying Germany with oil. After the bombing of Pearl Harbor, Getty devoted himself to managing the Spartan Aircraft Company, which built airplane parts for the U.S. military. Getty later purchased several other major oil companies, cementing his fortune between 1949 and 1953 by drilling for oil in the neutral zone between Kuwait and Saudi Arabia.

By 1957, Getty, worth close to a billion dollars, was dubbed the richest man in America by *Fortune* magazine. When one of his grandsons, J. Paul Getty III, was kidnapped in 1973, he originally refused to pay any ransom. After Getty's death, Texaco bought out the Getty Oil Company.

5. George Herbert Walker Bush (b. 1924)

The son of Wall Street banker and Connecticut senator Prescott Bush, George H. W. Bush grew up in tony Greenwich and attended prep schools and Yale University. But he moved his family to Texas, where he joined a successful oil-drilling equipment firm.

In 1953 Bush founded the Zapata Corporation to drill for oil in the West, and became president of its offshore division. In 1963, the firm merged with another company to become Pennzoil, and by the time Bush sold his interest in 1966, he was a multi-millionaire. Rumors persist that Zapata acted as a CIA front company for the failed 1961 Bay of Pigs invasion of Cuba. We'll never know: the Securities and Exchange Commission destroyed some of Zapata's filings—accidentally, they say.

In 1966, Bush won a seat in the U.S. House of Representatives, and later served as United Nations representative, chair of the Republican National Committee (during Watergate), and head of the China office under Richard Nixon. He was also CIA chief under Gerald Ford. As veep to two-term president Ronald Reagan, Bush was a key player in the Iran-Contra scandal but was never charged with any wrong-doing.

Bush won the presidency in 1988 (and Dick Cheney was his secretary of defense), but four years later, with the economy tanking, he lost his reelection bid to William Jefferson Clinton. Eight years later, his son, George Walker Bush (b. 1946), became president, with Dick Cheney as his veep. Bush Jr. was also a former oilman, although his level of success in the world of oil was not high. Strangely, Bush Jr. recently called for an end to this nation's "addiction to oil."

5 Ways to Decorate Your Undisclosed Location

Are you experiencing a national emergency? Is your survival a matter of international importance? If you've recently entered the Vice-Presidential Protection Program, you may want a few tips to make your undisclosed bunker feel more like a home. Following are five tips on how to duck and slipcover.

1. First, assess your space. Is it aboveground? Is it underground? If above, it's probably worth the expense of custom blackout shades. Plywood boards across windows do nothing for a room and can lead to a dark, depressed feeling. Also, very little goes with plywood that's even worth mentioning. If you're underground, consider investing in a dehumidifier, and just because there are no windows doesn't mean you can't have drapes. Faux windows can open up a room and add a cheery touch when you're 100 feet below sea level.

2. Are your lodgings more detainee than luxury? Spruce

them up with a fresh coat of paint and some vibrant area rugs. Think color, color, color!

3. Personalize. Add a few throw pillows, pictures of loved ones, a gun rack, or even something that reminds you of home, such as an oil well, which will always give you that warm and cozy feeling.

4. When you're finally feeling at home, you'll want to consider entertaining. More than likely there are several Secret Service agents who would love a special night. Light snacks, a game of charades, and a few scented candles will be more than enough to make the evening in your undisclosed location a night to remember, even if no one can ever talk about it.

5. Don't be surprised if you shed a nostalgic tear when it's time to leave your undisclosed location—especially if the world has been leveled by a nuclear conflagration or you have to face criminal charges. On the other hand, it's always possible that you've become president.

Dick Cheney was walking along the beach found a bottle. When he rubbed it, the bottle released a puff of smoke and a magical sound, and presto! A genie appeared.

"I will grant you the customary three wishes," said the genie. "But there is one condition. I am a Democratic genie. So, for every wish you make, every Democrat in the country gets the wish as well—only double."

Dick Cheney thought about this for a while. "For my first wish, I would like a hundred million dollars," he announced.

Instantly the genie gave him a Swiss bank account number and assured the man that one hundred million dollars had been deposited. "But every Democrat in the country has just received two hundred million dollars," the genie said.

At that, Dick Cheney pouted. "That's just wrong," he said.

"That's the deal," the genie said. "Now quickly, your second wish."

"Well, I've always wanted a Ferrari," Dick Cheney said.

Instantly a Ferrari appeared. "But every Democrat in the country has just received two Ferraris," the genie said. "And what is your last wish?"

Despite getting what he wanted, the very notion that Democrats were getting twice as much was genuinely hurting the vice president. What was the point of having what you wanted if other people had twice as much of it? That's not the Republican way.

So Dick Cheney thought deeply for a moment, and came up with a third wish. "I think it's time I donate a kidney," he said.

"According to doctors, George Bush has the lowest heartbeat ever recorded by someone in the White House. Well, second lowest. Dick Cheney got his down to zero a couple of times."

—Jay Leno

"Not to worry, the man who was shot left the hospital today, and they said he was in good condition—a little gamey, but still moist."

—Bill Maher

10 Most Destructive Lies
Dick Cheney Has Told

Dick Cheney has taken the art of fabrication, equivocation, and prevarication to new heights—or lows. Whether he's on the podium, across from your favorite anchor, or anywhere else for that matter, few people can match his ability for fiction told with such stern, self-assured gravitas. Here are ten of his more frightening deceptions.

1. "Simply stated, there is no doubt that Saddam Hussein now has weapons of mass destruction."
   —August 26, 2002, Veterans of Foreign Wars National Convention
   Truth: Despite years of searching since the invasion Dick Cheney advocated, no weapons of mass destruction have ever been found in Iraq.
2. "[Iraq is] the geographic base for the terrorists who have had us under assault now for many years, but most especially on 9/11."
   —September 14, 2003, *Meet the Press*
   Truth: The CIA's September 21, 2001, President's Daily Briefing, which Dick Cheney received,

said there was no link between the Iraqi government and the 9/11 attacks, a finding confirmed by every major investigation of the attacks since.

3. "I continue to believe—I think there's overwhelming evidence that there was a connection between al-Qaeda and the Iraqi government. . . . I'm very confident that there was an established relationship there."

      —January 22, 2004, NPR's *Morning Edition*

   Truth: The same September 21, 2001, CIA President's Daily Briefing said there was no Iraqi link to al-Qaeda, a finding also confirmed by every major investigation since.

4. "My belief is we will, in fact, be greeted as liberators."

      —March 16, 2003, NBC's *Meet the Press*

   Truth: The U.S. military personnel who entered Iraq have not been greeted as liberators. Instead, they have been the victims of an increasingly mortal insurgency that has already killed 2,300 U.S. soldiers and wounded an additional 17,000.

5. "I can say that we, in fact, are consistent with the commitments of the United States that we don't engage in torture. And we don't."

      —December 18, 2005, ABC News *Nightline*

   Truth: Retired U.S. Army Colonel Larry Wilkerson, who served as former secretary of state Colin Powell's chief of staff, told CNN on November 20, 2005, "There's no question in my mind that we did [torture]. There's no question in my mind that we may be still doing it. There's no question in my mind where the philosophical guidance and the flexibility in order to do so originated—in the vice president of the United States' office. His implementer in this case was Donald Rumsfeld and the Defense Department."

6. "I have no financial interest in Halliburton of any kind and haven't had, now, for over three years."

   —September 21, 2003, NBC's *Meet the Press*

   Truth: During his tenure as vice president, Dick Cheney has been receiving deferred compensation from Halliburton and holds company stock options valued at nearly $8 million. Although the Cheneys have assigned future profits from their stock options to charity, the deferred compensation creates a potential conflict of interest—if the company goes bankrupt, it will be unable to pay.

7. "I had a firm policy that we wouldn't do anything in Iraq, even arrangements that were supposedly legal." (Of his time as Halliburton CEO.)

   —July 30, 2000, *This Week,* ABC News

   Truth: The Washington Post reported on June 23, 2001: "According to oil industry executives and confidential United Nations records, however, Halliburton held stakes in two firms that signed contracts to sell more than $73 million in oil production equipment and spare parts to Iraq while Dick Cheney was chairman and chief executive officer of the Dallas-based company."

8. "I don't have anything to do with the contracting process, and I wouldn't know how to manipulate the process if I wanted to."

   —Fox News Radio, January 2004

   Truth: On June 14, 2004, the *Los Angeles Times* reported that the vice president's office helped overrule an army lawyer's blocking of a $7 billion no-bid contract to Halliburton in March 2003. Regarding a $1.9 billion contract in 2002, *The New York Times* wrote on July 14, 2004: "The Pentagon sought and received the assent of senior Bush administration officials, including the vice president's chief of staff, before hiring the Halliburton Company to develop secret plans for restoring Iraq's oil facilities."

9. "Conservation may be a sign of personal virtue, but it is not a sufficient basis for a sound, comprehensive energy policy."

—April 30, 2001, Annual Meeting of the Associated Press

Truth: On the heels of the large bulk of scientific research, government scientists used the results of a three-year study to show that a conservation program sponsored by the White House could accomplish both a decrease in dependency on fossil fuels and a reduction in pollution.

10. "The amount of land affected by oil production [in the Arctic National Wildlife Refuge] would be two thousand acres, less than one-fifth the size of Dulles International Airport."

—April 30, 2001, Annual Meeting of the Associated Press

Truth: Drilling for oil isn't a surgical activity that damages only the land upon which drilling takes place. Dick Cheney ignores the fact that most of the damage comes from creating the miles of roads and pipelines that will run through the protected lands to serve the drilling. The vice president is also being deceptive when he implies that all of the drilling will take place in one concentrated spot. In fact, the U.S. Geological Survey predicts the ANWR drilling is "expected to occur as several accumulations rather than a single large accumulation."

5 Strangest Lies Dick Cheney Has Told

1. "The first time I ever met you was when you walked on the stage tonight." (Of his opponent, Senator John Edwards.)

   —October 5, 2004, Vice-Presidential Debates

   Truth: As video footage and photographs that played endlessly in the days following the debate showed, Dick Cheney had met Edwards at least three times prior—at a prayer breakfast in 2001, at Elizabeth Dole's swearing-in ceremony in 2003, and backstage at *Meet the Press*—and, the odds are, many other times that weren't caught on camera.

2. "I think they're in the last throes, if you will, of the insurgency."

   —June 20, 2005, *Larry King Live*

   Truth: In the months that have followed, the insurgency in Iraq has flared to bloodier, more violent heights.

3. "No. I never said that." (About whether he ever said that it was "pretty well confirmed" that a meeting

took place between 9/11 hijacker Mohamed Atta and Iraqi intelligence.)

   —June 17, 2004, CNBC

   Truth: On *Meet the Press,* December 9, 2001, Dick Cheney told Tim Russert, "It's been pretty well confirmed that [Mohamed Atta] did go to Prague and he did meet with a senior official of the Iraqi intelligence service in Czechoslovakia last April."

4. "I can tell you that the government had absolutely nothing to do with it." (In response to Senator Joseph Lieberman's comment "I'm pleased to see, Dick, that you're better off than you were eight years ago.")

   —October 5, 2000, Vice-Presidential Debate

   Truth: As Jane Mayer's February 16, 2004, piece in *The New Yorker* details: "In fact, despite having spent years championing the private sector and disparaging big government, Dick Cheney devoted himself at Halliburton to securing government funds. In the five years before Dick Cheney joined Halliburton, the company received a hundred million dollars in government credit guarantees. During Dick Cheney's tenure, this amount jumped to $1.5 billion."

5. "[I] would have obviously been happy to serve had I been called."

   —March 1989 Senate Confirmation Hearing for Secretary of Defense

   Truth: In the five years Dick Cheney was eligible for the draft, he did everything he could to avoid serving, including applying for five deferments. It worked. He never served any time in the military.

9 Lies Dick Cheney
Hasn't Told . . .

. . . yet.

1. "The Syrian people will welcome us as liberators."
2. "Detaining people alleged to be terrorists without a warrant is absolutely constitutional. After all, if they are terrorists, they aren't American citizens and therefore can't expect the protection of what remains of the Constitution."
3. "We have irrefutable proof that Iran was responsible for 9/11 and that the Iranian government has opened its arms to Osama bin Laden and is offering him and al-Qaeda sanctuary."
4. "We have irrefutable proof that France was responsible for 9/11 and that the French government has opened its arms to Osama bin Laden and is offering him and al-Qaeda sanctuary."
5. "Of all of the acres in the Grand Canyon, and that is quite a bit, drilling operations will affect only approximately one-hundreth of the total available acreage,

just that tiny strip of water near the bottom that you can barely see anyway."

6. "Halliburton can rebuild Iran. They are well placed and have done this type of work before—and very inexpensively, I might add."

7. "You are mistaken. Most certainly the vice president has the power to declare war. It's part of the Patriot Act."

8. "Senator Clinton, with all due respect to your opinions regarding the performance of my duties as vice president, I don't recall having ever met you."

9. "I didn't die two years ago."

10 Ways to Tell If You're Dick Cheney

1. When you go hunting with your lawyer, you shoot him and
   a. apologize
   b. make him apologize
2. When you see a gay couple you
   a. wish them well
   b. pretend they're your lawyer
3. You have a strong feeling that the United States Constitution should apply to everyone in
   a. the country
   b. the country except you
4. You think pollution
   a. should be strictly regulated
   b. doesn't exist
5. You think that art
   a. should be federally subsidized
   b. doesn't exist

6. You think immigrants crossing the border illegally are
   a. part of a much larger issue that must be resolved with fairness on both sides
   b. target practice
7. You believe that the government should stay out of people's lives
   a. always
   b. always, except when it comes to marriage, pregnancy, sex, the church, prayer, library books, public education, and the country's official language
8. When it comes to women's health, you believe that
   a. women can be trusted to make decisions about their own bodies
   b. only white men can be trusted to make decisions about women's bodies
9. You think prayer
   a. should not be allowed in school
   b. should always be allowed, unless it's a prayer to Buddha or Allah, in which case it should never be allowed
10. As far as the Constitution goes
    a. the ACLU should be congratulated for defending it
    b. the NRA should be congratulated for defending it

Score: If you even thought about picking (a) just once, not only are you about to be wiretapped, you are *not* Dick Cheney and you never will be.

One day a blind rabbit and a blind snake met each other in the forest. These animals were very old, and so neither of them could remember just exactly what kind of animal they were. They decided to feel each other's bodies and come up with the answer.

The rabbit said, "You touch me first."

The snake agreed, and he started feeling the rabbit. "Well," he said, "you have fur all over, and you have a little cotton tail, and two long ears . . ."

The rabbit said, "I know! I'm a rabbit! Hurray!"

Then the rabbit felt the snake. He said, "Okay, you're slimy all over, you have no backbone, and you have this little forked tongue . . ."

The snake screamed in horror, "Oh no, I'm Dick Cheney!"

"Rumors are that the reason Dick Cheney didn't say anything about the hunting accident for about twenty-four hours was because he had been drinking. And I'm thinking, well, jeez, he was probably drinking when we planned the invasion of Iraq."

—David Letterman

"Today, President Bush says he is standing behind the vice president. Way behind him."

—Jay Leno

7 Movies to See with Dick Cheney

1. *The Shooting Party*
2. *The Shootist*
3. *Shooting Fish*
4. *Shoot the Moon*
5. *Shoot the Piano Player*
6. *Shoot to Kill*
7. *A Shot in the Dark*

5 Vice Presidents Worse Than Dick Cheney

Joshua Hammer

Joshua Hammer, an award-winning foreign and war correspondent for Newsweek, *has served as the magazine's bureau chief in Nairobi, Buenos Aires, Berlin, and Jerusalem. Currently* Newsweek's *correspondent at large, he is based in Cape Town, South Africa. Hammer is also a contributor to* Mother Jones, The New Republic, *and the* Smithsonian, *and the author of two books,* Chosen by God: A Brother's Journey, *a 2000 finalist for the* Los Angeles Times *Book Award, and* A Season in Bethlehem: Unholy War in a Sacred Place. *His third book is coming out in September:* Yokohama Burning: The Deadly 1923 Earthquake and Fire That Helped Pave the Way to World War II. *However, according to his two children, he is best known as a good father.*

Think that ours is the world's worst veep? Here are five challengers to the title.

1. Vice President Joyce Mujuru of Zimbabwe
   Joyce Mujuru is infamous Zimbabwe President Robert Mugabe's favorite hatchet woman. The wife of Mugabe's former military chief of staff, Mujuru

signed an amendment to the notorious Public Order and Security Act in February 2006 that increases the punishment for writing or saying anything unflattering about Zimbabwe's dictator from one to seven years in prison. It also raises the fine from one million to ten million Zimbabwean dollars, although that penalty may prove less harsh than it sounds. Thanks to the regime's disastrous economic policies, including the seizure without compensation of white-owned farms (Mujuru and her husband own at least two of them), inflation has run at about 1,000 percent a year. That makes the new fine currently worth U.S.$68 on the black market.

2. Yang Hyong Sop, Vice President of the Presidium of the Democratic People's Republic of Korea

For pure human misery, Yang Hyong Sop, who is married to Dear Leader Kim Jong Il's aunt, and his Politburo pals take the rice cake. According to human rights groups, the North Korean Communist regime bears direct responsibility for a famine that has caused the deaths of three million men, women, and children in a population of about twenty-two million. *The Economist* writes that North Korea has "produced seven-year-olds who are on average 8 inches shorter and 22 pounds lighter than their potential South Korean playmates." In addition to presiding over mass starvation, Yang Hyong Sop has played a key role developing North Korea's nukes and hawking missiles and other weaponry to such countries as Libya, Iran, Egypt, Pakistan, Syria, and Nigeria.

3. Vice President Farouk al-Sharaa of Syria

In October 2005 al-Sharaa, a longtime loyalist to the Assad family, was accused of lying to United

Nations investigators who were examining high-level Syrian complicity in the murder of former Lebanese prime minister Rafiq Hariri. Al-Sharaa had claimed in a letter to the U.N. commission that Syrian president Bashar al-Assad and Hariri had a general discussion about Syrian-Lebanese relations in a meeting in August 2004; in fact, according to a highly placed U.N. informant, Assad threatened during the meeting to "crush" Hariri. In February 2005 Hariri was blown to bits along with twenty others in a massive truck bomb explosion on a Beirut street. The scandal led to the suicide of Syria's interior minister Ghazi Kanaan, but somehow earned al-Sharaa a mysterious promotion from foreign minister to vice president. He is in line to become Syria's leader if Bashar al-Assad resigns or dies.

4. (Former) Vice President Jacob Zuma of South Africa

Like Dick Cheney, Zuma came to the number two job in the government with impressive bona fides. The African National Congress leader joined the struggle against apartheid in 1960 and spent a decade imprisoned on Robben Island with Nelson Mandela. But Zuma, known for his lavish lifestyle, was fired by President Thabo Mbeki last year after documents surfaced showing that a friend and financial adviser, Shabir Shaik, paid him $178,000 in exchange for helping him secure a lucrative military contract. The Durban High Court judge who convicted Shaik on all counts last year described his relationship with Zuma as "generally corrupt." While waiting for his own corruption trial to start, Zuma this month pled not guilty to charges that he'd raped an HIV-positive AIDS activist at his Johannesburg home in November. He could be sentenced to life imprisonment if convicted. (Zuma claims he's been set up by political rivals.) Unlike Dick Cheney, whose favorable rating has rapidly dwindled, the charismatic Zuma remains highly popular among the ANC masses.

5. (Former) Vice President Taha Yassin Ramadan of Iraq

This thuggish Saddam loyalist is now on trial in Baghdad, along with his former boss, on charges of involvement in the execution of 147 people in the Shiite village of Dujail after an assassination attempt against Saddam in 1982. Known as one of the dictatorship's enforcers, Ramadan also allegedly played a key role in crushing the Shiite uprising in southern Iraq in 1991 and in killing thousands of Kurds in the north in 1988. When Ramadan was appointed Iraq's industry minister in the 1970s, the diehard Baathist reportedly told colleagues: "I don't know anything about industry. All I know is that anyone who doesn't work hard will be executed."

7 Groups You Can Join to Fight Dick Cheney

1. Halliburton Watch (www.halliburtonwatch.org/home .html)

   Mission: To provide essential information on important topics neglected by the mass media and policymakers that will encourage citizens to become active and engaged in their communities.

   The tagline says it all: "Wanted, Halliburton, for bribery, fraud & trading with the enemy." HalliburtonWatch.org is a project of Essential Information, a nonprofit, tax-exempt organization, and the Center for Corporate Policy, a nonprofit, nonpartisan organization working to stop corporate threats to democracy. Ardent Dick Cheney watchers get their own "Cheney Cashing In" section, which includes coverage of ethics laws violations, crooked Arthur Anderson accountants, and an entire Dick Cheney–Halliburton chronology. You can keep on top of the latest news, access a vast Halliburton historical archive, and take action, including offering anonymous information useful to law enforcement or investigative journalists about Halliburton.

2. People for the American Way (www.pfaw.org)

Mission: To meet the challenges of discord and fragmentation by affirming "the American Way" via full support of pluralism, individuality, freedom of thought, expression, and religion, a sense of community, and tolerance for others.

What could Dick Cheney hate more than a one-stop-shopping website for those hoping to fight domestic spying, ban torture, and stop the war in Iraq, while supporting civil liberties and equal rights for all? PFAW was founded in 1981 by Norman Lear, Barbara Jordan, Father Theodore Hesburgh, and Andrew Heiskell to counter the growing clout of the right wing, and especially of televangelists such as Jerry Falwell and Pat Robertson. Since then, its effective use of television ads has shaped public opinion on a variety of political and social issues, helping to block the appointment of Robert Bork to the Supreme Court and to counter the Christian coalition and Clinton impeachment. PFAW continues to be an essential resource for communicating with local legislators and media outlets; letter writing is one of the best ways to participate and support PFAW's mission.

3. CODEPINK (www.codepink4peace.org)

Mission: To activate, amplify, and inspire a community of peacemakers through creative campaigns and a commitment to nonviolence.

Launched in 2002 with a four-month vigil in front of the White House, this women-initiated, grassroots organization boasts over 250 local chapters, from Fayetteville, Arkansas, to Boise, Idaho, and internationally from Brazil to Iran; its mailing list reaches over 60,000 people every week. CODE-PINK, which plays off the Bush administration's color-coded Homeland Security Advisory System, is based on compassion and is a call for women and men to "wage peace." Rejecting fear-based politics, it calls for policies based on compassion, kindness, and a commitment to international law.

4. American Civil Liberties Union (www.aclu.org)

Mission: To defend and preserve the individual rights and liberties guaranteed to every person in this country by the Constitution and laws of the United States.

The ACLU, founded in 1920 by Roger Baldwin, Crystal Eastman, Albert DeSilver, and others, is a nonprofit, nonpartisan group that has grown from a roomful of civil liberties activists to an organization of more than 400,000 members and supporters. The ACLU has litigated against many of the vice president's trademark policies, including the trampling of constitutional rights by the Patriot Act, the denial of due process for detainees and their abuse in Guantonamo, and the unconstitutional surveillance of U.S. citizens without warrant by the National Security Agency (NSA). There's an ACLU affiliate in every state and Puerto Rico that handles requests for legal assistance, lobbies the state legislatures, and hosts public forums throughout the year.

5. Sierra Club (www.sierraclub.org)

Mission: To promote the exploration, enjoyment, and protection of the earth's wild places, the responsible use of the earth's resources; it enlists and educates humanity to protect and restore the quality of the natural and human environment.

The club is America's oldest, largest, and most influential grassroots environmental organization, with more than 750,000 members who work to protect the environment. The club has been tenacious in its criticism of what it calls Dick Cheney's big-energy giveaway, also known as the Cheney Energy Task Force for rewriting National Energy Policy. Bringing light to the fact that the task force was made up of behemoths like Enron and Exxon who wrote the resulting *National Energy Policy*, the Sierra Club fought the vice president all the way to the Supreme Court. Through the club's vast network dedicated to congressional lobbying and grassroots action, members have the opportunity to get involved with local chapters, be part of a national network of environmental advocates, and gain the satisfaction of helping preserve irreplaceable wild lands and wildlife.

6. WesPAC (www.securingamerica.com)

Mission: To elect Democrats to the White House and Congress in order to implement new policies that will restore our nation's security and prosperity.

Founded by General Wesley Clark in 2004 after his unsuccessful presidential bid, WesPAC's philosophy is as anti–Dick Cheney as it gets: A truly secure America demands sound, wise leadership and a renewed commitment to the values that have made our nation great—service, integrity, and accountability. Clark has thirty-four years of service in the United States Army, including a stint working for Dick Cheney and Donald Rumsfeld in the Ford White House. He ultimately rose to the rank of four-star general as NATO's Supreme Allied Commander, Europe. After his retirement in 2000, he became an investment banker, author, and commentator, and was soon drawn into the Democratic presidential race in 2004. The WesPAC site has a grassroots action center where you can help support the troops, stop global warming, and gain access to media contact information.

7. MoveOn.org (www.moveon.org)

Mission: To offer the means for busy but concerned citizens to find their political voice in the midst of big-money-big-media politics.

This group was started in 1998 by Joan Blades and Wes Boyd, two Silicon Valley entrepreneurs who shared a deep frustration with the partisan warfare in Washington, D.C., and especially the wasteful spectacle of the Clinton impeachment. Now with over 3.3 million members across the country, MoveOn.org works aggressively to realize the progressive vision of our country's founders. You can become directly involved in the political process by keeping up with a slew of current campaigns, making donations, or signing petitions that go directly to the source—including Congress and the media.

5 Bad Dogs Speak Out on Cheney

R. D. Rosen, Harry Prichett,
and Rob Battles

R. D. Rosen, Harry Prichett, and Rob Battles are co-authors of the best-selling Bad Dog *and* Bad Cat *(with Jim Edgar), and the forthcoming* Bad Baby. *Rosen is an Edgar-winning mystery novelist and author of the word* Psychobabble *(and the book of that name). His comedy has appeared on PBS, HBO, CBS, and, with Harry Prichett, on NPR's* All Things Considered. *Prichett has written and performed for the improv groups Chicago City Limits and Radio Active Theater, had an off-off-Broadway one-man show, and appeared on television and in film. Battles has written and produced for public radio and is currently an extremely important executive in commercial television promotion.*

See more Bad Dogs in the book Bad Dog: 278 Outspoken, Indecent, and Overdressed Dogs *(Workman Publishing).*

"Guns don't shoot friends in
the face. Vice presidents do."

NAME: Wally

HOBBY: Making quail feather
collages

"He makes me so damn mad."

NAME: Duncan
HOBBY: Reupholstering

"Five deferments? I guess he was just waiting for the right war."

NAME: Bodie

HOBBY: Creating dioramas of famous executive-branch mishaps

"I'm not moving till Cheney's
out of office."

NAME: Ellie
HOBBY: Finding a new hobby

"Don't argue with me. I know a clown when I see one."

NAME: Burt

HOBBY: Juggling draft deferments

7 People Who Hate Dick Cheney More Than You Do

1. Joseph Wilson

   Wilson was a United States foreign service diplomat between 1976 and 1998, and from 1988 to 1991 he was the deputy chief of mission at the U.S. Embassy in Iraq. He was hailed as "truly inspiring" and "courageous" by George H. W. Bush after sheltering more than one hundred Americans at the embassy, but Wilson became a punching bag for the current administration after he wrote an explosive op-ed piece for *The New York Times* in July 2003 titled "What I Didn't Find in Africa," about his February 2002 fact-finding mission to Niger, which debunked claims that Iraq was buying yellow-cake uranium. Wilson's piece ticked off the vice president so much he allegedly instructed his then chief of staff, Lewis "Scooter" Libby, to reveal Wilson's wife, Valerie Plame, as an undercover CIA agent. Special prosecutor Patrick Fitzgerald indicted Libby on charges related to the outing. Wilson makes no bones about cheering Fitzgerald on.

2. Representative John Murtha

Representative Murtha has well served his country both in the military and in Congress. One of only 131 people who have spent more than thirty years in the House, he remains very popular at home, Pennsylvania's Twelfth Congressional District. Murtha's decorated thirty-seven-year military career in the U.S. Marine Corps includes the American Spirit Honor Medal, the Bronze Star with Combat "V," two Purple Hearts, and the Vietnamese Cross of Gallantry.

In November 2005, Murtha, who had initially supported the Iraq war, became one of its most vocal opponents, loudly calling for the immediate withdrawal of American troops. Dick Cheney then said of his former friend Murtha's change of heart, "The president and I cannot prevent certain politicians from losing their memory, or their backbone—but we're not going to sit by and let them rewrite history." Murtha responded by calling Dick Cheney's position on Iraq "a flawed policy wrapped in illusion," and said of Dick Cheney himself, who avoided serving in Vietnam in the 1960s: "I like guys who've never been there who criticize us who've been there. I like that. I like guys who got five deferments and [have] never been there and send people to war and then don't like to hear suggestions about what needs to be done."

3. Maureen Dowd

Bestselling author of *Are Men Necessary?* and a Pulitzer Prize winner for her series of columns on the Bill Clinton–Monica Lewinsky scandal, Maureen Dowd has had her Dick Cheney antennae on high alert since she began serving as correspondent in the *New York Times* Washington bureau in 1986. Now a regular columnist for the *Times,* Dowd regularly blasts the vice president with her acerbic writing style, using nicknames like "Shooter in Chief" and "Vice" in her column. And in a 2004 interview, Dowd said: "Dick Cheney is really . . . the villain of Bushworld, and a very dark force."

4. Representative Henry Waxman

Henry Waxman has represented California's Thirtieth Congressional District since 1975 and has long been a leader on health and environmental issues, including universal health insurance, AIDS, and women's health research and reproductive rights. Waxman has been doggedly lobbying various federal agencies to follow the trail of corruption, nepotism, and cronyism involved in the second Iraq war; he has also led the battle to uncover the truth behind why Bush cited forged documents in his State of the Union address in 2003, which has subsequently shed a harsh spotlight on Dick Cheney—who was reportedly aware of the forged document almost a year before Bush's speech. Waxman has also drawn attention to the vice president's role as the former chairman and CEO of Halliburton and how the company has benefited from wars in Bosnia, Afghanistan, and Iraq.

5. Arianna Huffington

A nationally syndicated columnist, Huffington describes herself as a "former right-winger who has evolved into a compassionate and progressive populist." She has created and lent her name to the highly successful Huffingtonpost.com, an online forum for some five hundred famous (and not so famous) bloggers such as Al Franken, Gore Vidal, and Representative John Murtha, but Huffington often saves the best lines for herself. She once told the right-wing Fox News channel, "I think Dick Cheney's an atrocious

Rick Santorum, Orin Hatch, and Dick Cheney were traveling together by car to a political fund-raiser in a remote part of the country. Their car broke down, and they were forced to seek shelter for the night at a nearby farmhouse.

The farmer welcomed them in, but cautioned them that he had only two spare beds, and so one of the trio would have to sleep in the barn, where the man kept his two farm animals.

After a brief but intense discussion, Rick Santorum agreed to take the barn. The others went to bed, but not more than a few minutes later, they heard a knock on the farmhouse door. The farmer and his guests all got up to answer it, and there they found Senator Santorum complaining that he could not sleep. There was a pig in the barn, he said, and it was making him too unhappy, because it reminded him of the fact that so many people called him a pig.

Orin Hatch then volunteered to sleep in the barn. But this time it was less than ten minutes before another knock was heard at the front door. There was Senator Hatch, who complained that there was a horse in the barn who kept defecating, and it reminded him of being in the Senate.

Dick Cheney, in desperation for a good night's rest, then agreed to sleep in the barn. This seemed like a good idea until a few minutes later, when another knock was heard. When the farmer answered the door, there stood the very indignant horse and pig.

"The U.S. Army confirmed that it gave a lucrative fire-fighting contract in Iraq to the firm once run by Vice President Dick Cheney without any competitive bidding. When asked if this could be conceived as Cheney's friends profiting from the war, the spokesman said 'Yes.' "

—Conan O'Brien

"Kind of a sad study out today that single women over the age of 35 are more likely to be shot by the vice president than to find a husband."

—Jimmy Kimmel

human being . . . and an atrocious vice president who has inflamed terrorists, who has created more terrorists than he has ever destroyed."

6. Patrick J. Leahy

A practicing lawyer until he was elected to the U.S. Senate in 1974, Leahy is Vermont's first Democratic senator and a highly popular national figure. As the ranking Democrat on the Senate Judiciary Committee, Leahy's chance meeting with the vice president on the Senate floor in 2004 became the stuff legends are made of: After Leahy expressed his displeasure over Dick Cheney's ties to Halliburton and President Bush's judicial nominees, the vice president shocked witnesses when he unceremoniously told Leahy to go "f**k yourself." The polite and gentlemanly Leahy kept his cool, but this infamous exchange, and Leahy's continuing inquiries into Halliburton, keep his anti-Cheney flames burning brightly.

7. Alec Baldwin

One of the most vocal and animated liberals in Hollywood, the star of *The Hunt for Red October* and *Beetlejuice* has had Dick Cheney's number since his first days in the White House. In his regular blog on the Huffington Post, Baldwin calls the "lying, thieving" Dick Cheney a "terrorist," an "oil whore," and "the worst vice president in U.S. history." Though often criticized for his vocal politics, Baldwin remains fiercely devoted to Democratic causes, regularly squaring off with far-right-wing personalities such as Bill O'Reilly. While Baldwin remains a highly sought-after character actor, he's suggested that he may give up acting to pursue political office in the near future.

9 Other Famous Dicks

1. Dick Whittington (1350–1423)

   The most famous Dick of yore, he was, according to the long-told fable, a penniless boy who ended up living in the house of his employer, a rich merchant. Dick then gave his beloved cat to the merchant as an investment in a sailing voyage; the cat heroically killed an infestation of rodents and was bought by the king, making Dick very rich and, eventually, the mayor of London (and the husband of the daughter of the rich merchant).

   In reality, there was indeed a Dick Whittington, but he was actually just a young man who lost out on his inheritance and went to London to learn the fabric trade; through hard work, he became a very wealthy exporter of wool and importer of silks and velvets. His fortune allowed him to lend large sums of money to the king, who was running a deficit. As thanks, the king allowed Dick to export his wool without paying the normal export taxes. (Oddly enough, this deprived the crown of revenue to pay off its loans and attendant interest.)

When Dick died, he left his great wealth to benefit the city of London. Today the charitable trust, which helps the poor, is still called The Charity of Sir Richard Whittington.

2. Moby-Dick (1851)

Call me Dick. Okay, Ishmael was the hero, but Moby-Dick was the big guy. Long story short: A leviathan is hunted by an obsessive-compulsive. For months, the whale misleads his pursuers with his secretive meanderings. The captain and crew of the whaling vessel *Pequod* seem unable to trap the elusive creature. They are caught up desperately seeking vengeance in a kind of psychological torture. Finally, Moby-Dick feints capture and drags his pursuers to their death. The whale is harpooned in the end, but he enjoys a hearty last laugh as everyone dies except the narrator. This is one Dick you don't want to fool with.

3. Dick Nixon (1913–1994)

The thirty-seventh president was the first one to resign from office. Nixon's tenure was highlighted by such achievements as creating the Occupational Safety and Health Administration (OSHA) and the Environmental Protection Agency (EPA), withdrawing from Vietnam, and becoming the first president to visit (what was then known as "Red") China.

Overshadowing these accomplishments were the resignation of his vice president, Spiro Agnew, for taking bribes; the secret bombing of Cambodia; and Nixon's involvement in the Watergate break-in and cover-up (the investigating grand jury referred to him as the "unindicted co-conspirator").

But don't forget that this Dick was also our thirty-sixth vice president. In 1952, he was only thirty-nine years old when he was elected with Dwight Eisenhower. During the campaign, rumblings arose that Dick had misappropriated funds for personal use, and his position on the ticket seemed shaky. Dick then took to the airwaves to give a complete accounting of the Party's funds and a trip through his personal spending and gifts received. In a particularly poignant moment, he revealed that he had been given a cocker spaniel named Checkers as a gift, but he couldn't return him (presumably in violation of federal law) because his daughters loved the dog too much. It was the most successful speech ever given by any Dick.

4. Dick of Dick and Jane® Fame (Published 1927 to 1965. Dick and Jane® is a registered trademark of the Addison-Wesley Educational Publishers, Inc.)

Both Dicks ran. This one was stopped in his tracks as the country foundered over the rise of the nuclear family, integration, feminism, and phonics.

Bucolic and happy until the 1960s, Dick and Jane (and Sally, see below), as well as their friends, lived a happy life, introducing us to one word at a time, called the "whole word method," repetitively and gradually building on that word. See Dick. See Dick run. See Dick shoot.

Then the academic world was rocked on its ears when it was suggested that the whole word method was overly simplistic, didn't allow for an appreciation of literature, and fostered sexist stereotypes as well. And in 1965, when the government started requiring better educational materials for underprivileged students (which actually included them in the subject matter), African Americans Pam, Penny, and Mike were born.

But the most tragic part of the story is Sally. The books were really about Sally, Dick, and Jane, but poor Sally, not part of the trademark, fell into the dustbin of history. See Sally fall.

5. Philip K. Dick (1928–1982)

Dick was an extremely well regarded science fiction writer, more studied and revered after his death than during his life. Although ignored by all but sci-fi addicts while alive, today his works are often found in American literature courses at universities around the country.

Dick was born a twin, but his sister died six weeks later. His parents divorced when he was five, and his mother took custody. He attended the University of California in 1949, but never graduated.

About eight years before his death, Dick had a series of visions, which have consumed his critics and acolytes. Whether they were brain-addled hallucinations, fakery, or divine communication, these visions gave him plenty of material to write about, and were certainly more interesting to his readers than his four marriages and his on-again, off-again schizophrenia diagnoses.

6. Dick Van Dyke (b. 1925)

English chimney sweep to Julie Andrews's Mary Poppins, Mary Tyler Moore's husband in his eponymous TV show, inventor of a flying car whose girlfriend is named Truly Scrumptious, this Dick has been a hardworking actor in television and movies for close to fifty years.

His latest stint as the wise Dr. Sloan in *Diagnosis Murder* proves you can never be too old to be a crime-fighting doctor, or at least play one on television.

Perhaps one of the least remembered but most truthful moments in network television occurred in 1974 when Dick, playing an alcoholic businessman in the movie *The Morning After,* revealed that he had just conquered his own alcoholism, a subject that wasn't normally discussed, especially in public.

Years of watching him tumble over his on-screen ottoman and then adroitly sidestep it have helped to make this Dick either much beloved or mildly irritating.

7. Dick Clark (1929–forever)

It was said that when the television show *American Bandstand* was on the air in the late 1950s, this Dick was more popular than the president—and the vice president named Dick as well. However, in 1959, a scandal erupted: Dick owned financial interest in a number of songs being played on his show. He was investigated by the Senate, which in the end found that Dick had done nothing illegal; the network ordered him to either give up his questionable investments (which he did) or leave the network.

This little hiccup hardly hindered Dick on his rise to creating a broadcasting empire, which includes such cultural bellwethers as *Super Bloopers & New Practical Jokes,* and *The World's Biggest Lies.*

8. Dick Tracy (1931–forever)

This Dick is an all-around good-guy cop who fights underworld figures such as Yogee Yamma, Flattop Jones, and Itchy Oliver. He first entered the world of crime fighting when he walked into a robbery in progress and watched the murder of his fiancée's father. For the past seventy-five years he has been relentlessly fighting the bad guys with his two-way wrist radio. He adopted a son who was a reformed thief, fathered a daughter, and has had his share of marital trials and tribulations, almost divorcing in the nineties, but love eventually triumphed. Although he is a comic book figure, many Americans think that Dick Tracy is actually the name of a real person.

9. Dick Cavett (b. 1936)

Born in Nebraska, this Dick studied acting at Yale and attempted a career as a stand-up comic before he found his niche as a television talk-show host in 1969. He has been on the air more or less since then with a couple of brief hiatuses. His success has arisen from his distinctive conversational style coupled with his idiosyncratic voice and dry humor.

He has also guest-starred on a number of sitcoms and movies and starred as the narrator in the Broadway revival of *The Rocky Horror Picture Show* for over a year. Dick has suffered from depression since he was in college and has been increasingly open about discussing it, as well as his treatment, in recent years.

Typical Dick witticism: "I went to a Chinese-German restaurant. The food is great, but an hour later you're hungry for power."

4 Ways to Recover from a Bad Speech Even If You've Just Shot a Man or Launched a War

Francis Wilkinson

Francis Wilkinson, a strategic communications consultant and speechwriter based in Nyack, New York, has advised numerous Fortune 500 corporations and Democratic political campaigns. Wilkinson's essays and articles have appeared in the opinion pages of The New York Times, The Washington Post, *and the* Los Angeles Times, *as well as in major publications such as* The New Republic, The New York Times Magazine, *and* Harper's. *A former National Affairs correspondent for* Rolling Stone, *Wilkinson is a recipient of a National Magazine Award, which he won in the Public Interest category.*

1. Relax. People respond to your demeanor and body language. One of the reasons Dick Cheney's favorability rating is lower than, say, Michael Jackson's, is that while both of these public figures do a lot of scary things—dangling babies from balconies, subverting the Constitution, and the like—only Dick Cheney looks as though he enjoyed committing the offense and would gladly do the same thing again in a jiffy.

I wouldn't say the goal here is to be more like Mike—just less like Dick. Are you angry most of the time? Prone to go off and shoot some poor old duffer in the face when things aren't going your way? Before you go onstage to deliver your speech, you need to practice it in front of a mirror, keeping an eye on your facial expressions and body language. If your presentation displays telltale signs of psychosis, it can be a turnoff to some audiences. So before you deliver your speech, do a little demeanor check. If you find yourself jabbing your index finger in the air and saying things like, "You talking to me?" then take a break, take a hike, take a deferment. Take five.

2. Enunciate. Speeches matter. In addition to being the complete embodiment of evil, Adolf Hitler knew a thing or two about working a crowd. He once said that every great movement in world history owes its rise to great speakers. The man valued the spoken word.

But to reach your audience, you've got to speak clearly. One reason Dick Cheney has such a hard time winning us over is his tendency to mumble. People have different reasons for mumbling. Some lack confidence. Others are telling an outrageous lie and would like to get it over with quickly. The vice president manages to mumble in such a way that it seems he has contempt not only for certain ideas ("democracy"), but for humankind. This is bad form.

When you stand at a podium, enunciate every word. It conveys respect for yourself, for the words you're speaking, and for your audience. I once asked a friend who coaches opera singers to pick the one pop singer who was most admired by the Verdi crowd. I expected her to say Frank Sinatra or Sarah Vaughn or some such. Her reply? "Willie Nelson. He enunciates beautifully." See? Even a cowboy can do it.

3. Self-deprecate. Your audience wants to like you. But you can help them along and help yourself, too, with a little self-deprecating comment at the outset of your speech. It's best if this comment is funny. But if you can't manage to be funny, at least get the self-deprecating part right.

   Here again, demeanor is key. If it looks like you're just going through the motions, the audience will recognize your halfhearted effort as a fraud. Instead of embracing the audience, you will have pushed them away; you'll have to work that much harder to win their affection, attention, and respect.

   So have a little fun at your own expense. No matter how bad a shot you are, you can still be a good sport.

4. Depart. Unless you've just declared World War III, it's tough to hold an audience's attention. As your own experience as an audience member surely confirms, most speeches are too long. There's no need to ramble. Just say what you have to say and get off the stage.

   In one sense, Dick Cheney has got this right. Since he rarely leaves his bunker, we're always interested to see what he looks like (is he twitching today?). Similarly, since he rarely speaks to the public, we tend to hang on every grunt emitted from his sneering lips. What was his message to that respectable, white-haired senator from Vermont on the Senate floor? "Go f**k yourself." If you want a short, concise, vehemently direct message, you can't do better than that. You couldn't pack more contempt in a tractor trailer.

Yet despite an obvious talent for terseness, the vice president still needs a bit of prodding to get off the stage. Long after the expiration of his usefulness, generously defined, to the Republic, he is still malingering behind the curtains. Don't be like Dick. When your time in the spotlight is up, do the right thing. Depart.

5 Things to Expect Dick Cheney to Do as Global Warming Intensifies

Eugene Linden

Eugene Linden is the author of Winds of Change: Climate, Weather, and the Destruction of Civilizations, *which was hailed by* The New York Times *for its "penetrating historical view," and by the scientific journal* Nature *for its in-depth research and verve. For many years Linden wrote about global environmental issues for* Time, *and he has contributed to publications ranging from* National Geographic *to* Foreign Affairs. *Linden's numerous awards include the American Geophysical Union's Walter Sullivan Award for excellence in scientific journalism. His website is eugenelinden.com.*

If climate turns out to be the weapon of mass destruction Vice President Cheney should have been worrying about, he has a problem. Let's say in the near future hurricanes, nor'easters, dust bowls, floods, crop failures, ice storms, and tornadoes are ruining the economy, and the voters are blaming Dick Cheney because he and President Bush dismissed the science behind the threat, ridiculed conservation (one of the easiest ways to immediately lessen greenhouse gas emissions) as a "civic virtue," and were champions of the fossil fuel industry. Dick Cheney may think he has big business on his side, but even before Katrina, many CEOs began joining the tree huggers. Even the evangelicals, whose leaders went enviro, called for action. So when the weather changes, what will Dick Cheney do?

1. Blame the Democrats. This is easy; it's what he always does, and they usually don't fight back. Dick Cheney will say that he and Bush inherited the problem from the Clinton administration (not mentioning that it was a Republican-controlled Congress that torpedoed action) and that the Bush administration actually cut oil use by the end of its second term, while it steadily went up during the Clinton years (expect him to gloss over the fact that supply disruptions due to civil war in the Middle East and a worldwide depression caused the decline).

2. He will claim that no one could have seen it coming. That strategy worked for a bit after Katrina—until those irritating videotapes and e-mails started surfacing. And the truth is, it's entirely possible that the vice president didn't see it coming: It's unlikely that any of the "experts" his administration consulted, ranging from science fiction writer Michael Crichton to the paid lackeys of the coal industry, mentioned that it might be a problem. (Don't expect him to acknowledge that the entire scientific establishment had been warning of the threat for fifteen years.)

3. He will argue that the Kyoto Treaty would not have helped, and that he and Bush were engaged in a search for the real way to deal with the problem, one that includes India and China. This one is tricky-

smart. It's true that Kyoto is vastly inadequate to the scale of the threat, but it could be made stronger. On the other hand, he will have to finesse that India and China are never going to join an effort on climate change unless the United States, with 25 percent of world emissions, shows leadership on the issue.

4. He will say the crazy weather is natural. Why not? That's what the naysayers have been saying whenever an ice shelf collapses. It's unlikely that Dick Cheney will mention that carbon dioxide, which has tracked temperature for millions of years, is now at higher levels than its been since Homo sapiens evolved (better for him to avoid evolution anyway).

5. Expect him to move to Canada. Washington will have a climate like Khartoum, and Vancouver will be the new San Diego.

Dick Cheney was filling out a job application when he came to the question, "Have you ever been arrested?"

He answered, "No."

The next question, intended for people who had answered in the affirmative to the last one, was "Why?"

Dick Cheney answered it anyway: "Never got caught."

"It turns out now that Dick Cheney did not have a license to hunt, and coincidentally, turns out we didn't have a license to go into Iraq."

—David Letterman

The vice president is standing by his decision to shoot Harry Whittington. Now, according to the best intelligence available, there were quail hidden in the brush. Everyone believed at the time there were quail in the brush. And while the quail turned out to be a 78-year-old man, even knowing that today, Mr. Cheney insists he still would have shot Mr. Whittington in the face. He believes the world is a better place for his spreading buckshot throughout the entire region of Mr. Wittington's face."

—*Daily Show* correspondent Rob Corddry

8 Ways Dick Cheney Secretly Controls Intelligence

1. Keep the President Clueless

   Keeping the president in the dark for eighteen hours about a shooting incident wasn't the first time the vice president has kept Bush clueless about historic matters. A more critical example emerged in the 9/11 Commission Report that detailed how the vice president, in the hour after the attacks on the World Trade Center and the Pentagon, told Bush a specific threat had been made on Air Force One when none had been made. While Bush spent the rest of the day evading the supposed threat, Dick Cheney assumed presidential authority, implying a call from the president had granted it to him. No such call took place.

2. Stack the Deck with Cronies

   Wherever you go in Dick Cheney's world, you meet his men. Donald Rumsfeld, who as secretary of defense has delivered us the Iraq war and torture at Abu Ghraib and Guantanamo, gave Dick Cheney his first job in the White House, working for Richard

Nixon. Paul Wolfowitz, undersecretary of defense for the first term of the Dick Cheney vice presidency as well as chief architect of the Iraq war and one of the principal proponents of preemptive war, dates back to Dick Cheney and Rumsfeld's anti-détente work in the Ford administration. Lewis "Scooter" Libby, Dick Cheney's chief of staff until his indictment on perjury charges, joined up with the vice president and Wolfowitz in their continuing anti-Soviet-détente work for the first President Bush. David Addington, general counsel to the vice president until he replaced the indicted Libby as Dick Cheney's chief of staff and chief architect of the administration's pro-torture policies, first caught the veep's favor as a young GOP congressional staffer on the Iran-Contra committee.

3. Ignore Dissent

Lawrence Wilkerson, chief of staff for Colin Powell while he was secretary of state, witnessed this firsthand. As Wilkerson told an audience at the New America Foundation in October 2005, "You've got this collegiality there between the secretary of defense and the vice president. And then you've got a president who is not versed in international relations—and not too much interested in them either. And so it's not too difficult to make decisions in this, what I call the Oval Office Cabal, and decisions often that are the opposite of what you thought were made in the formal [decision-making] process."

Or as former National Security Council expert on Iraq Kenneth Pollack told Seymour Hersh in his October 27, 2003, *New Yorker* article, Dick Cheney and company "dismantled the existing filtering process that for fifty years had been preventing the policymakers from getting bad information. They created stovepipes to get the information they wanted directly to the top leadership. They always had information to back up their public claims, but it was often very bad information."

4. Plant Your Own Findings

In other words, create intelligence, and use it as justification for actions. Before the Iraq war, Dick Cheney funneled money to Iraqi Shia Muslim politician Ahmad Chalabi and his Iraqi National Congress (INC), and the INC provided sources stating that Saddam had weapons of mass destruction, including nuclear capabilities. Even though the CIA and German intelligence disqualified the veracity of these sources, the vice president continued to use them as justification for policy.

5. Hide Things That Don't Fit

If facts get in the way, hide them. Former senator Bob Graham, the ranking Democrat on the Senate Intelligence committee before the Iraq war, detailed in his November 20, 2005, *Washington Post* editorial how key dissent contained in the classified version of the CIA's National Intelligence Estimate (NIE), the most important intelligence document in the buildup to the war, was omitted from the unclassified, public version of the NIE. The experience forced him to "question whether the White House was telling the truth—or even had an interest in knowing the truth."

6. Punish Those Who Disagree

When army head General Eric Shinseki told the Senate Armed Services committee that the Iraq war would take a minimum of 400,000 troops, Paul Wolfowitz, in front of the same committee, dismissed Shinseki's estimate as "wildly off the mark." Shinseki was then functionally relieved of his duties eighteen months before his scheduled retirement. And when former ambassador Joseph Wilson dared to question the validity of the Niger memo asserting Saddam's nuclear capabilities, Dick Cheney, many people believe, instructed his then chief of staff, Lewis "Scooter" Libby, to leak the identity of Wilson's wife, Valerie Plame, as a CIA agent to the press. When Ahmad Chalabi, the vice president's man in Iraq, started to question the administration's Iraq policy, a warrant was issued for his arrest by the U.S. military.

7. Keep It Secret

No administration has ever classified more documents (including reclassifying documents previously declassified), and no administration since Richard Nixon's has argued as insistently for executive privilege. The leading advocate of this secrecy has been Dick Cheney's right-hand man, David Addington. On the vice president's behalf, Addington has defended—all the way to the Supreme Court—Dick Cheney's right to withhold information about his energy task force, largely suspected of blueprinting, prior to 9/11, a plan for control of Iraq's oilfields after a U.S. invasion.

8. Dissemble

To this day Dick Cheney still draws connections between Saddam Hussein and the attacks on 9/11, even though he and the president were briefed just days after the attack that there was no such connection—as other members of the Bush administration have admitted. The vice president also claims that Saddam had nuclear, chemical, and/or biological warfare capabilities and that the Iraqi dictator had ties to al-Qaeda—all claims about which he has specific contradictory evidence.

7 Haiku as Written by Dick Cheney

1

We like to hunt quail
I thought your face was feathers
So sorry blood beak

2

I am pretty sure
(buckshot blood snickers bad press)
It was not a bird

3

I am loved by George
George has served me loyally
So glad I picked him

4

Hillary Clinton
Weapons of mass destruction
Sharp pains in my chest

5

Wise, gray-haired statesman
Experience and knowledge
Hey! Go f**k yourself!

6

Oligarchy? Sure
Plutocracy? Yup, you bet
Democracy? Feh

7

Katherine Harris
A state, once blue, becomes red
Let me count the ways

6 Ideas for Campaign Reform

Doris "Granny D" Haddock

Doris "Granny D" Haddock, ninety-six, walked across America in her ninetieth year to support campaign finance reform. Earlier in her life she organized a successful effort to stop planned H-bomb testing in Alaska. She ran for the U.S. Senate in New Hampshire in 2004 when no Democrat would oppose the powerful Republican incumbent. She did so to speak out against Bush-Cheney policies. Partially as a result of her speeches, New Hampshire was the only swing state that swung from Bush-Cheney in 2000 to Kerry-Edwards in 2004. She is the author of Granny D: You're Never Too Old to Raise a Little Hell *(Random House).*

Keeping car keys away from a drinker or a gun away from a psychopath are important strategies for personal survival. For national survival, we should consider keeping campaign cash away from fellows like Dick Cheney. Here are some survival strategies to get us through until the day when we have wise leaders again:

1. Get the public financing of elections passed in more states and at the federal level. Maine, Arizona, and

Connecticut led the way. Support organizations in working on that reform in the other states. Check out publiccampaign.org and just6dollars.org and get involved.

2. Support candidates who will foil Dick Cheney and his gang in Congress. The Internet makes it possible for millions of small donors to overcome the oligarchy of major donors who distort public policy and harm us all. It's easy to complain, but let's start putting our time and dollars where our mouths are.

3. Use the citizen ballot initiative process in the states that provide that tool to expand the conflict-of-interest laws, which make it illegal for public officials to take action when it affects the people and organizations who bankroll their political careers. Then let's force that reform at the federal level. Would that create gridlock on K Street and Capitol Hill? Oh, dear. One bill would certainly get through, and that is the public financing of campaigns.

4. Until we get an expansion of the conflict-of-interest laws, let's start talking about "moral conflicts of interest." It's simple: Just attend public hearings in city halls, state capitols, and on the Hill, and stand up and say, "Point of order, Mr. Chairman: I believe Senator Snort's political career is beholden to the industry involved in this matter, which gives him a moral conflict of interest. He should recuse himself."

Now, when one person does that, you have a kook escorted from the room. When several people do that every day, you have a crisis and a movement for reform. Mr. Cheney's gang cannot prosper in that environment, and it can begin whenever people are brave enough and organized enough. Perhaps one of the good-government organizations will grow the *cajones* to warm up to this kind of serious action while there is yet some ice at the North Pole. The D.C. jail is a rather decent place, I can tell you. It is, in other words, time to start making other people red in the face with the ammunition of their own donations.

5. The oil barons who have taken up residence in the White House feel safe in their assumptions that we mass millions will continue to consume and live lives dependent on cheap energy and imports. As long as we do, they are indeed safe. Our best strategy for disempowering Mr. Cheney and his gang for the remainder of their terms is to plan a better world ourselves, to live it in our own lives, and to consider national strikes against consumption to get our battle lines in proper formation.

6. The most powerful people in America are the children. If they would dare to march on Washington from across the nation to stop global warming, torture, the destruction of free public education, and the like, Mr. Cheney would run faster than a Texas lawyer in duck season.

7 Steps to Creating Your Dick Cheney Protest Record

John Hartmann

John Hartmann began his career in the mailroom of the William Morris Agency and later served as WMA liaison to Colonel Tom Parker, Elvis Presley's manager. A veteran agent, personal manager, and record executive, Hartmann has worked with such performers as Sonny & Cher, Buffalo Springfield; Peter, Paul & Mary; Crosby, Stills, Nash & Young; Eagles; Jackson Browne; Poco; America, and many others. Hartmann, cofounder of Jake Records and president of Topanga Pictures, an independent film production company, also serves on the board of Smartpaper Networks, a tech company he founded in 2000. He currently teaches a course about the recording industry at Loyola Marymount University in Los Angeles.

If you want to be a pure artist, write a song, walk naked in the woods, and sing it to the birds. But if music for change is your goal, here are seven active steps you can take.

1. Write the song. The structure for a song was set in stone thousands of years before one was ever written down. Find one you like and follow its paradigm. Include verses, a chorus, and repetition with variation.

Discover a musical hook, and discover the rhythm. And above all, try to find the phrase that pays, that golden verbal nugget, so rich in veracity that it cannot be denied.

2. Perform the song. Test it on any audience that will listen. If you don't play an instrument, find a musician and hum it to him or her. The strengths and weaknesses will emerge in the crucible of action. The truth is always clear and easily understood. Once the song is fixed in a reproducible medium it is considered copyrighted. Call the American Society of Composers, Authors, and Publishers (ASCAP) or Broadcast Music Inc. (BMI), and they will tell you how to protect your intellectual property. It is now yours forever. Don't sell it.

3. Record the song. We are living in the Music Renaissance. Recording in the digital age is neither expensive nor esoteric. There is a Pro Tools Studio in every computer and a band in every garage. Producers are lurking on every college campus, and in most high schools as well. Go to a gig and talk to any musician under the age of twenty-five. If he loves the song, he will do it. It will cost you nothing but time.

4. Make a record. Come up with the cover art. Get on Photoshop, gather some images that speak to your message, and put them together. Collect all the credits that honor the creative people involved. Take your product to one of the manufacturing companies that create compact discs. Each will cost you less than two bucks. Now you are a record company with an album to sell. Maybe you are an artist as well.

5. Release your record. To make your record available for sale, you must handle some legal issues. All the

A tourist entered an old, musty antique store in Boston. There, while looking around, he spotted a very lifelike, life-sized bronze statue of a rat. The tourist couldn't find a price on the rat, but the detail work was so excellent the tourist decided he had to buy it for his wife, who loved small animals.

The tourist cleared his throat loudly, and from behind a curtain of Chinese beads appeared a wizened old man.

"I see you like my rat," the old man said.

"Absolutely," said the tourist. "How much do you want for it?"

"You can have it for ten dollars," said the old man, "but the story behind the rat will cost you a thousand dollars."

The tourist thought the old man was crazy but he didn't care. "I don't want the story," he said. "I'll just buy the rat."

Happy with the deal, the tourist left the store and started walking down the street. Soon he realized that some real rats were following him. He turned around. Crawling out of alleys, appearing from sewers, jumping down from windows, more and more rats began to appear.

Becoming frightened, the tourist started walking faster and faster. But the herd of rats kept growing, and when the tourist next turned around, he saw at least a hundred rats following him, all squealing, jumping, and running.

The tourist broke into a run himself, but he could barely outpace the rats, who now numbered in the thousands. Finally, as the tourist approached the harbor, he took the statue and heaved it as far as he could into the ocean.

To his surprise, all the rats jumped into the ocean, too, and were never seen again.

The tourist then walked back to the antique shop, where he found the old man rubbing his hands together, as though waiting for him.

"I knew you'd come back for the story," said the old man.

"Screw the story," said the tourist. "I came back to see if you had a bronze Republican."

"To the vice president's credit, he did own up to it. On Fox News he said the fault was his, he can't blame anybody else. Boy, it's amazing, the only time you get accountability out of this administration is when they are actually holding a smoking gun."

—Bill Maher

"The guy Cheney shot is a Texas lawyer. While he was lying there on the ground he actually handed himself his own business card."

—Jay Leno

rights are protected by law, and the profits must be shared with your partners (which most people end up having). It's best to get an entertainment attorney to handle the array of contracts that protect the equities involved. They're in the phone book.

6. Promote your record. The traditional avenues are burdened with enormous costs, from payola to legitimate radio promotion. However, you have a tool at your disposal that is infinitely more powerful than AM and FM radio combined: There are thousands of websites on the Internet where marketing systems prevail. Offer your record for free and link it to every possible connection that might listen or pass it on to others.

7. Sell your record. The most effective way to recoup your costs is to sell a CD. This brings us back to performing live. You can start today in the street. Pass the hat and offer albums for sale. With 100 percent of the profit, you will recoup your investment in no time. If there is a band in your garage, move it into the local clubs. When you find fans, collect their e-mails and nourish interactivity with them. They will tell their friends.

My last piece of advice: Now there is no excuse for you to absent yourself from action. If you follow these simple instructions, you can have a voice in the future of your planet. You can stand up against injustice, tyranny, and corruption. With the song in your heart, you can change the world.

8 of Dick Cheney's Favorite Foods

1. Plame-Broiled Chicken
2. Iraq of Lamb
3. Field Greens with Crude Oil and Vinegar
4. Ken Lay's Potato Chips
5. Baked Alaska Pipeline
6. Scooter Pie
7. Yellow Cake Uranium
8. Harry Whittington

8 Reasons Why Not All Oilfield Workers Support Dick Cheney

George Lattimore

After studying geology and physics at Colgate, Lattimore drove to Oklahoma to work as a roughneck on drilling rigs. He then worked at Enserch, a Dallas-based oil company, and later joined the consulting engineering firm of Grace, Shursen, Moore & Associates, where he supervised oil and gas projects as well as drilling operations at Los Alamos National Laboratory and at the Grand Canyon. Since 1983 Lattimore, who has written articles for the Society of Petroleum Engineers *and* World Oil *magazines, has worked internationally with such companies as British Gas, Chevron, and Halliburton on drilling projects in diverse locations, including Yemen, Sudan, New Guinea, Indonesia, and the former Soviet Union. Presently, Lattimore is operations manager for a gas development project in central Mozambique.*

For the most part, oilfield workers (OFWs) have little in common with Dick Cheney. He isn't really an oilfield guy; he was a political science major who became a politician. He has never worked on a rig or in a refinery, has never put together an engineering plan, has never done any of the other things OFWs do. He got on the board of Halliburton because of political contacts, and then he nearly destroyed it with the Dresser Industries acquisition, which brought on the asbestos mess and near bankruptcy for Big Red (oilfield vernacular for Halliburton). Big Red was once a proud American company, founded by a guy who came up through the ranks: Earl P. Halliburton. Dick Cheney was the first non-oilfield-related CEO, and the culture of loyalty built over the years started to break down under him.

Here's more:

1. He disobeys rules. This is contrary to OFW culture. Why? Drilling rigs are dangerous places where people can be maimed and killed. (So are hunting grounds.) Rigs have a no-tolerance rule with respect to alcohol. Drinks are not allowed on-site, plain and simple. Rotational workers are not even allowed to drink during off hours. Folks on remote and dangerous sites have to depend on each other for mutual protection. Anyone who considers himself above the rules can't be tolerated for the sake of the whole.

2. He is not a straight shooter. Oilfield workers don't waffle about bad news; they tell it like it is. Accidents are reported immediately, and steps taken to diagnose the cause and prevent future occurrences. Rigs are dangerous places even with best practices in place and there is no place for obstructionists.

3. He doesn't plan ahead. Oilfield projects must be planned exhaustingly from beginning to end, complete with contingency plans. We don't take big actions without thinking ahead—it's embarrassing, costly, and potentially dangerous. Iraq wasn't planned. The previous engineering types running Halliburton would have known that.

4. He's hurt our image overseas. Since the Iraq invasion, Americans working and living internationally have never been less secure. Where we once felt respect, we now encounter a great deal of hatred. Our image of holding the moral high ground has been destroyed and our failings have empowered our adversaries.

5. He hurts the environment. Not all OFWs hate nature. Just because we're oil workers doesn't mean we don't have kids; we want a clean and healthy place to raise them. How can you have energy policy meetings without environmental advocates looking beyond today's stock prices to tomorrow's air and water quality?

6. Oilfield workers can like fuzzy bears and dislike fuzzy math. Look at the case for Arctic Wildlife Refuge drilling. It's being sold "to lessen our dependency on foreign oil." The refuge contains between four and twelve billion barrels of recoverable oil. The United States uses twenty million barrels per day. If the refuge oil were used to supply 5 percent of that requirement, it would be depleted in twelve years, using the lower estimate. Does a 5 percent boost for a dozen years significantly reduce our dependence?

7. What's good for Exxon on a large scale isn't necessarily good for OFWs. For the most part, we are folks trying to make a living for our families. Most of us are not part of Bush's base; the administration's tax cuts for the 1 percent don't trickle down here.

8. The bad reputation Dick Cheney has saddled OFWs with among nonconservatives isn't deserved. No-bid contracts or not, companies are not standing in line to work in Iraq. Folks are dying over there, and the people doing the work aren't bad guys, just folks earning a living. Modern oil reserves are found in some pretty

inhospitable places: jungles, deserts, stormy oceans. But the vice president has helped make us look like demons. For years my twin daughters wouldn't admit to their friends that their father worked for the bad guys. (But I think that they, and my wife, still love me.)

5 Editorial Cartoons
About Dick Cheney

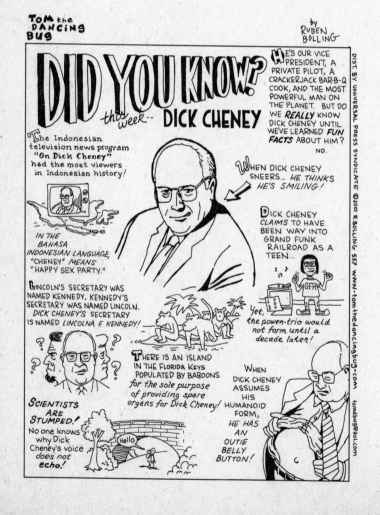

© Grimmy, Inc. "Reprinted with permission of King Features Syndicate"

"Reprinted with permission of King Features Syndicate"

5 Flawed Vice Presidents

While few Americans can name more than a handful of vice presidents (ever heard of Thomas Hendricks, Henry Wilson, or George Clinton?), the following men have made their mark on history. Unfortunately, they did so by failing to live up to the standards of their job.

1. Aaron Burr, Vice President Under Thomas Jefferson (1801–1805)

   Although Founding Father Alexander Hamilton and Aaron Burr had been on good terms for many years, after Burr defeated Hamilton's father-in-law for the New York Senate in the 1790s, the relationship turned frosty. It only worsened when Burr and Thomas Jefferson were placed on the same presidential ticket. Their ticket won, but contrary to expectations, Burr decided that he wanted the presidency, not the vice presidency. At the time, the House of Representatives made the final choice between president and vice president. Popular opinion expected

Jefferson to get the nod, but Burr refused to capitulate. After thirty-seven votes, and thanks to the efforts of Hamilton, Jefferson was awarded the office, and Burr's reputation was stained by having not been a team player.

Meanwhile Hamilton's criticisms of Burr were growing in intensity as well as quantity. At one dinner party, Hamilton supposedly outdid himself in his tirade, and Burr demanded a retraction and an apology. He didn't get one. So Burr challenged Hamilton to a duel.

They met in Weehawken, New Jersey, early in the morning on July 11, 1804, counted off, and fired. Hamilton's bullet missed, possibly on purpose, but Burr's did not. Hamilton, gravely wounded, died the next day. Burr, charged with murder, was never tried.

Later, Burr allegedly attempted to organize an independent country from the states that would later form the lower Louisiana Purchase. Burr was charged with treason, but was eventually acquitted when no witnesses were produced. Eventually he practiced law.

2. John Breckinridge, Vice President Under James Buchanan (1857–1861)

Politically, Breckinridge was a difficult person to pin down. Slavery was the primary issue during the 1856 presidential campaign; Breckinridge was known for giving speeches that spoke directly to his audience—to a fault. If he spoke to abolitionists, he was pro-abolition. If he spoke to anti-abolitionists, he was anti-abolition.

Tensions increased between the North and South until the breaking point neared. Breckinridge wanted and expected his native Kentucky to join the

South. When it failed to do so, he joined the Confederate army and landed a high position in the secessionist government. After Richmond, the capital of the Confederacy, was captured by the Union, Breckinridge escaped and headed toward Florida, procuring a small boat and pushing off into the Atlantic Ocean. Twenty-eight days later, covered with insect bites, swollen from too much sun and seawater, he landed in Cuba.

Meanwhile, back in the United States, the government charged Breckinridge with treason. But when President Andrew Johnson declared a general amnesty for secessionists, Breckinridge was allowed to return to Kentucky.

3. Schuyler Colfax, Vice President Under Ulysses S. Grant (1869–1873)

Shortly after becoming veep, Colfax made known his intention of seeking higher office. His lack of interest in his current position helped persuade his boss, Ulysses S. Grant, to choose another man as veep for his second term. This proved a good move, for soon thereafter the Crédit Mobilier scandal broke.

Crédit Mobilier was a company set up by Union Pacific Railroad to bid on railroad construction projects. Somehow, the company seemed to win a number of those projects without even bidding. These projects were often funded by big federal subsidies, and they were often funded for much more than they actually cost.

About the time Colfax took office, Congress started making noises about investigating where all its money was going. Colfax's name quickly arose, but he denied ever having known of Crédit Mobilier.

A truck driver in Texas used to find it funny to scare people on the side of the road by driving right at them and then veering away at the last possible minute. He liked watching the look of horror on their faces as he came near, and the way they scampered out of the way like mice.

He was not a nice man.

But one day, while driving, he spotted a priest hitchhiking along the side of the road. Given that he'd spent the last few years terrifying so many people, the trucker thought he should do something nice so he could get into heaven. He pulled his rig to the side of the road and rolled down the window.

"Where are you going, Father?" he asked.

"About ten miles down the road to the old church," the priest replied.

"Great!" the driver said. "I'll give you a lift.

The priest climbed into the passenger seat and the truck driver continued on his way.

Not more than five minutes later the truck driver saw another man walking down the road. As usual, his instinct was to scare the guy by almost hitting him. He started to veer the truck toward the side of the road, but then he realized that the man was Vice President Dick Cheney, and besides, the priest probably wouldn't find it as much fun as he did.

So at the last minute the driver managed to swerve away from the vice president. Strangely, he could have sworn he heard a thumping noise. He couldn't figure out why. Still, he turned to the priest and said, "I'm very sorry, Father. I just missed hitting the vice president."

"That's okay," said the priest. "I got him with the door."

"Cheney says he feels terrible about what happened. The man he shot was his friend and if he could, he'd give him the central processing unit right out of his own heart to make up for it."

—Jimmy Kimmel

"What I don't understand about this whole thing is that the guy who got shot, this is his statement today, he said, 'My family and I are deeply sorry'—his face got in the way— 'for everything the vice president and his family had to go through this weekend.' Wow, that is one loyal Republican. He also referred to the buckshot wound in his face as 1,000 points of light."

—Bill Maher

Charges were made to the contrary, however, especially when his bank account showed large deposits matching Crédit Mobilier dividend payments in exact amounts and dates.

In what must have been a memorable bit of testimony, Colfax, trying to justify the payments, said that one morning a (conveniently dead) supporter's check just happened to waft in through the window on a breeze, and just happened to be on the same date and for the same amount as one of the dividend payments.

No one bought this. But since it was close to the end of his term, Congress let it go, as Colfax's political career was doomed.

4. Spiro Agnew, Vice President Under Richard Nixon (1969–1973)

Agnew was the popular Republican governor of Maryland when he was chosen to run as vice president, mostly because he was considered an attractive candidate who would stay out of Nixon's way. Not only did he not stay out of Nixon's way, Agnew embarked on a remarkable speaking career, continuously condemning his constant critics.

His use of words was staggering. Some of his best hits: "nattering nabobs of negativism," "hopeless, hysterical hypochondriacs of history" and "pusillanimous pussyfoots." He can't claim to have come up with these on his own (for that we can thank his speechwriters, William Safire and Pat Buchanan), but his performance was sheer fire—for a time.

No one will ever know what would have happened to Agnew's vocabulary if the Watergate scandal hadn't intervened, along with revelations concerning

Agnew's failure to pay taxes prior to his vice presidency. As Agnew's troubles were a nice temporary foil for the press's interest in Watergate, the Nixon administration let Agnew take the bullets, and take them he did. Indicted for accepting bribes when governor of Maryland, and for tax evasion, Agnew pleaded no contest to the charges and was convicted and fined, but not jailed.

Agnew later professed that he was innocent of the charges, claiming he was forced to plea-bargain by Nixon's handlers. He died on September 17, 1996.

5. William Danforth Quayle, Vice President Under George Herbert Walker Bush (1989–1993)

He never committed a crime; he was never indicted; he never betrayed the country. He was a loyal second in command to his boss. He campaigned hard and fought for his party.

However, Dan Quayle also made it clear that you didn't have to be an A, a B, or maybe even a C student to become vice president of the United States. Quayle has been very protective about releasing his academic record. However, one professor did offer this insight: "Dan Quayle was one of the few people able to get from the Deke [fraternity] house to the golf course without passing through a classroom."

And of course, when asked, Quayle was unable to spell *potato,* adding an *e* to the end of the word. But it wasn't just his spelling. It was his mouth. Even the current president has not (yet) matched the former veep for his classic malapropisms, misquotes, and boggled thoughts. To wit: "I have made good judgments in the past. I have made good judgments in the future." "Republicans understand the importance of bondage between a mother and child." "I am not part of the problem. I am a Republican."

Perhaps best of all, during a speech in Tennessee, he mangled the motto of the United Negro College Fund: "What a waste it is to lose one's mind. Or not to have a mind is being very wasteful. How true that is."

Yes, how true that is.

5 Ways to Stay Alive If You Suspect Your Date Is a Dick Cheney Sympathizer

Laurie Notaro

New York Times *bestselling author Laurie Notaro has written five books, including* The Idiot Girls' Action-Adventure Club, I Love Everybody (and Other Atrocious Lies), *and* We Thought You Would Be Prettier. *Raised in the dusty Barry Goldwater stronghold of Phoenix, Arizona, she was run out of town after refusing to drive a Hummer, erect a W monolith in her front yard, and sign a document that stated the sentence "Fool me once, shame on—shame on you. Fool me—you can't get fooled again" made perfect sense. Under the cover of night, she fled to the safety of Eugene, Oregon, with her* Harper's-*subscribing husband, although her ears still bleed and she often weeps if she hears the term* exit polls.

He arrives absolutely on time, opens the door for you, pulls out the chair, and smiles warmly, but it doesn't take long for you to suspect that something isn't quite right. There were hints, certainly; he picked you up in his Yukon XL (needing to refuel twice before you reached the restaurant), dropped the term *blame game* seven times in as many minutes, and mentioned that the appetizer gave him "heartburn that felt like a fifth heart attack."

But for a split moment you see it, as plain as the zipper scars on Dick Cheney's chest, and there is no denying it. The steely, beady, pigeonlike stare of one of them. *Them.*

While you realize that some Republicans are a little more human in their DNA double helix (Scott Baio, Krusty the Clown), this kind, the Dick Cheney Sympathizer, is of a different breed altogether. If Republicans had frequent-liar miles, his kind would be Platinum Elite, sit in first-class every time, ask for seconds of anything that's free, and leave a mess in the sky potty for someone else to clean up. Before you know it, he'll be leaning over the table to suck out your soul like a cat hovering over a helpless infant. Within days, you'll be shopping at Wal-Mart, chanting "It *is* hard to put food on my family!" and trying to figure out ways to get Nelson Mandela back into prison. He is evil upgraded, ranked even higher on the Dark Force creationism ladder than Lord Voldemort's Death Eaters.

Now, you could run, but to him that only makes you prey, much like a small, woodland creature, and therefore the Dick Cheney instinct will kick in and you'll be spending the night in the ER with an intern hovering over you with a pair of tweezers picking buckshot out of your jaw and neck. And that's only if you get away and don't end up separated into Ziploc bags at the bottom of a Deepfreeze by tomorrow morning. You need a plan.

1. Distract him by cooing, "Is that your gun and its correlating concealed-weapon permit, or are you just happy to see me?" and then slip silently away when he has to actually take a moment to check.
2. While in line for movie tickets, mention repeatedly to your date and stay on message that "Ron Silver is the

finest actor of this or any generation! When is the next Ron Silver movie coming out? I must know! I must know!" When he attempts to get an answer from the ticket person who is confused because he has never heard of Ron Silver, seek sanctuary in a foreign movie with subtitles. He will never find you there.

3. After an hour-long lecture on the trials and tribulations of being a business executive, your date finally asks you about your occupation, to which you answer, "Oh, I work at Brewster-Jennings & Associates, you know, doing a little of this, little of that. But it's a little boring now that my office pal Valerie P. quit. There's no one to go to lunch with. Now, where's that waiter with check? It's taking longer than a military deferment!" It's guaranteed the next stop you make will be at your curb, and you'll have to open the car door for yourself.

4. In the middle of dinner, become alarmed and shriek, "Red Alert! Red Alert! Maureen Dowd is hovering right behind you with a tape recorder!" and then call a cab after you've watched your date scramble out of the restaurant like Gollum, although it takes him approximately eighteen minutes and several three-point turns to unpark his land schooner and flee.

5. Should your date become too comfortable and make the mistake of confusing your fear with arousal, immediately hold up a clove of garlic and a recycling bin to repel him and cover all bases, whether they are merely vampiric or Republican.

8 Steps to Take If You Believe the Government Is Spying on You

X

X is an American intelligence operative whose identity cannot be revealed.

Paranoia is not a bad thing, especially when you are challenging the status quo. Be safe, have fun, follow all the advice given below, and you may live to see the next election.

1. Never look or act guilty—anywhere, anytime, with anyone about anything. In fact, don't let your personality ever control your actions; you don't want to stand out in a crowd. In my case, I have always been a counterintuitive spy. I say that because by nature I'm an extrovert, and for the most part, introverts make better spies because they can control their external emotional behaviors more easily than an extrovert. So I always try to calm myself before engaging in any social interactions that might bring unwanted attention.

   On the other hand, there have been times when I purposely acted like a buffoon so those following me would think me too careless to be an intelligence officer.

2. Do not ever use your cell phone, computer, Black-Berry, or any other downloadable product for anything that might seem suspicious to those whose job it is to be professionally paranoid.

    The world of technology changes so rapidly that even intelligence services have a hard time keeping up with the best ways to protect themselves from being spied on. For example, for very small amounts of money, you can now link your computer via an online Web service to a satellite and take photographs, not only of buildings, but also of individuals entering or leaving a building. Hundreds of cameras currently focused on New York's Times Square are so powerful they can read the label on the back of designer dresses. You must assume, no matter where you go in the public domain, that you are being observed.

3. Always use public telephones (and never for more than forty-five seconds once connected) if you must discuss anything confidential.

4. Library computers are supposedly protected under the Patriot Act. Don't believe it.

5. Don't trust the services and companies that promise to protect your privacy. Some are capable of preventing most intrusions into your private life, but many of those same companies are paid extremely high figures to allow certain individuals, and agencies, to have a peek.

6. Beware of new friends who seem overly eager to get to know you better. Do not let them in your home, office, computer, or any other place that contains personal information (especially about them).

7. Keep those in need of financial assistance (including current friends, family members, and acquaintances) at a distance, especially if they are loyal to the government you may be suspected of questioning. People needing money will betray a friend or family member as fast as the idea forms itself in their minds.

8. If you're foreign-born, you've got an additional problem—like it or not, you stand out. One way to obviate the issue: Act like an American as much as possible. Even if you're not a foreigner, you may be considered the next-closest thing by the government if you have many foreign friends. Remember guilt by association? I do. While trying to develop internal contacts in a war-torn country, my own agency suspected me of being a double spy simply because I spent a great deal of social time with a few individuals I was trying to recruit.

12 Places to Go Online

6 Liberal Political Blogs

Given the mainstream media's increasingly conservative bent, and the general lack of nonconservative news sources, more and more people are checking out the Web for their news. There are many good sites, including Raw Story and Political Wire, as well as blogs by Steve Clemons, Joe Conason, Matt Yglesias, James Wolcott, Pam Spaulding, Josh Marshall, Oliver Willis, and a host of others. (See this book's site—TheDickCheneySurvivalBible.com— for a larger list.) But here are six sites that are particularly good for finding news that hasn't been censored by the administration.

1. Daily Kos
   www.dailykos.com
      Now an ancient four years old, this brainchild of Markos Moulitsas Zúniga is one of the granddaddies of liberal-leaning blogs; it's a good first stop for anyone looking to get a quick feel for what's happening

in the political scene. A true mark of Kos's meteoric success: Conservatives loathe this site. The mainstream media isn't very kind to it either.

2. My Due Diligence
www.mydd.com

Started in 2001, then empty for a year and restarted in 2004, bloggers Jerome Armstrong and Chris Bowers "provide their own analysis and commentary on campaigns, elections, and world affairs." The site provides some excellent long-form analysis and frequently features outspoken guest bloggers. Armstrong and Zúniga (Kos, above) recently teamed up to write *Crashing the Gate,* an analysis of progressive politics.

3. The Washington Monthly
www.washingtonmonthly.com

A magazine as well as an online source, *The Washington Monthly* delivers well-written and well-researched stories from excellent writers, but its online heart is Kevin Drum's Political Animal, a blog that breaks news as well as comments on already-broken stories.

4. Eschaton
www.atrios.blogspot.com

Headed by Duncan Black, a thirty-two-year-old "recovering economist living in Center City Philadelphia," this blog has been online since 2002. Can break news and post interesting stories, but perhaps it's best known for the long, rambling, and often fascinating threads posted by contributors.

5. Crooks and Liars
www.crooksandliars.com

Billing itself as an online virtual magazine in addition to the blogging, Crooks and Liars, written by John Amato, contains fresh daily audio and video clips. Much of what it posts goes viral very quickly.

6. AmericaBlog
   www.americablog.blogspot.com

   A solid take on progressive politics, as written by John Aravosis, a Washington-based writer who has created many successful websites, including StopDrLaura.com and Matthew Shepard Online Resources. Like the other sites, AmericaBlog also features various guest bloggers.

6 Websites That Laugh at Dick Cheney

These won't give you any solid information, but you might end up smiling, which is more than the administration will make you do.

1. Quail Hunting School
   www.quailhuntingschool.com/flash.php

   Try to get ten quail in the allotted time after having downed (at your choice) either no beer, one beer, two beers, or "lots." If you manage to hit the flying quail instead of the flying Harry, you'll get a certificate of completion and the satisfaction of knowing your skills are better than you-know-who.

2. Dick Cheney's Got a Gun
   www.bobrivers.com/audiovault/downloads/cheneyvid.asp

   Animated music video to an original song of the same name. Unrated. Contains one quick disturbing image of the vice president with his fly open.

3. Dick Cheney Goes Ahead with Folsom Prison Concert
   http://cheneyplaysfolsom.cf.huffingtonpost.com

Covering a Johnny Cash song in his own vice-presidential way, this is basically just an audio clip, but a pretty humorous one. Pay special attention to his self-introduction—you might almost swear it was Suzanne Pleshette.

4. I'm in Love, I'm All Shot Up
   www.huffingtonpost.com/paul-hipp/cheneys-victim-sings_b_15948.html

   Not to be left out, Harry Whittington has an Elvis-style comeback song to the Folsom Prison concert. Includes photo of Harry in sequined red jumpsuit.

5. Texas Takedown
   www.jadekite.com/texastakedown.html

   Flash game where, as Dick Cheney, you try to hit as many lawyers as you can. It's relatively easy to bag a virtual barrister, but please don't try this outside of cyberspace.

6. Dick Cheney Quail Hunt
   http://dickcheneyquailhunt.cf.huffingtonpost.com

   The basic idea is to click shoot when you see the quail (which looks more like a mallard duck). Crudely drawn and a little frustrating trying to actually shoot the quail. Perhaps it's programmed in that you can't actually ever hit a quail. After all, most hunters can't.

9 Songs on Dick Cheney's iPod

1. *Your Cheating Heart* (Hank Williams)
2. *Lies Lies Lies* (Thompson Twins)
3. *Sympathy for the Devil* (Rolling Stones)
4. *I've Got the Power* (Snap)
5. *More More More* (Andrea True Connection)
6. *Just Can't Get Enough* (Depeche Mode)
7. *When Will I Be Loved* (Linda Ronstadt)
8. *Opportunities (Let's Make Lots of Money)* (Pet Shop Boys)
9. Everything by Gerry and the Pacemakers

4 Ways to Tell If Your Husband Is Turning into Dick Cheney—and What to Do About It

Terry Real

Terry Real, the bestselling author (I Don't Want to Talk About It: Overcoming the Secret Legacy of Male Depression *and* How Can I Get Through to You? Closing the Intimacy Gap Between Men and Women*), is a family therapist whose work has been featured in numerous academic journals and media outlets. He offers lectures and workshops throughout the country and maintains a private practice in the Boston area, where he lives with his wife and two sons. For more information on his work, visit www.terryreal.com.*

1. He brings a shotgun to bed and yells, "Pull! Pull!"
    Response: Inform him that yelling "Pull" is only for skeet shooting. If he's after bird, he needs to squeeze gently.
2. He occupies your child's elementary school by force, fires everyone, and then brings in Halliburton to run the cafeteria.
    Response: Ask if there's a spot for you on the payroll.

3. He tells your neighborhood minister to go f**k himself!

   Response: Let him know diplomatically that although in some places (bus station urinals, the locker room of the Forty-second Street Y) vulgarity may be just the thing, there are other places (the U.S. Senate, an emergency room) where most people expect more refinement.

4. At the slightest sign of tension in the family, he retires to an undisclosed wine cellar somewhere on your property.

   Response: You might consider leaving him there.

4 Steps to Impeachment

Why bring up this topic? No special reason. It just never hurts to be informed about these sorts of things, because you never know when an impeachable offense will be dropped in your lap.

1. Know What Impeachment Means

    You can impeach a vice president or you can impeach a witness. *Impeaching public officials* means you are trying to remove them from office by bringing charges based on their conduct while in office. *Impeaching witnesses* means you are questioning their credibility during a court proceeding. Unless you're a lawyer, the only definition you care about now is the first one.

2. Know Your Constitution

    Article II, Section 4 of the Constitution states: "The President, Vice President and all civil Officers of the United States, shall be removed from Office on impeachment for, and Conviction of, Treason, Bribery, or other high Crimes and Misdemeanors."

Bribery and treason, no problem. But what are high crimes and misdemeanors? Controversy reigns over the exact definition. Violation of public trust? Abuse of office? Injuring the country to profit an individual or a group? Or, as Gerald Ford said, "Whatever a majority of the House of Representatives considers it to be at a given moment in history." You'll need to have a pretty strong idea what it is that someone has done wrong, and you better be right.

3. Know Your House of Representatives

It's in the House where the charges constituting impeachment are laid out. A resolution for impeachment will be created and referred to the Judiciary Committee, which makes an initial determination on whether or not there are sufficient grounds for impeachment. If so, the resolution will be turned into the Articles of Impeachment containing all the specifics of the alleged misconduct. These articles are then put before the entire House. The House debates and votes. A simple majority of the representatives then present is all you need to move forward. The House will also choose managers from among its members who will present the articles to the Senate.

4. Know Your Senate

The Senate is where the action is. The proceedings are basically a trial. The Senate acts as the jury, the House as the prosecution, and the vice president as the defense. After the trial, the Senate deliberates in private and then votes on each of the charges contained in the Articles of Impeachment. The voting is done in an open session and by roll call, with each senator's name being called out and his or her vote noted in full view of everyone in the Senate. Conviction requires a two-thirds majority of a quorum, that being "those mem-

One evening, Dick Cheney was hunting in a remote part of the Rockies. Somehow he managed to shoot a duck, and he started climbing over a fence onto a field to retrieve it. As he was doing so, an old farmer pulled up in his pickup truck and jumped out.

"Hey, what are you doing on my property?" the farmer asked.

"Picking up this duck I just shot," Dick Cheney said.

"Well," said the old farmer, "that duck is on my side of the fence, so now it belongs to me."

Dick Cheney looked surprised. "Don't you know who you're talking to?" he asked.

The farmer shook his head. "I don't know and I don't care," he said. "Just give me my duck."

"I'm Dick Cheney, vice president of these United States. And if you try to keep me from taking this duck, I will destroy you, your family, and everything that is dear to you."

"Well," said the farmer, "in this jurisdiction, the only law that matters is the three-kicks law."

"I don't know that one," Dick Cheney said.

"It's pretty simple," the farmer responded. "First, I get to kick you three times. Then, when I'm done, if you're able to get back on your feet and kick me back three times, the duck belongs to you."

Dick Cheney thought about it, and figured that because he was an ornery guy, and the farmer was far older and scrawnier, he could take the man. "I agree," he said.

At that the old man kicked Dick Cheney hard right in the groin. Then, as Cheney fell to the ground, the farmer kicked him even harder in the face. Then, as the vice president lay panting in the dirt, the farmer kicked him as hard as he could in the ribs.

After catching his breath, Dick Cheney gradually stumbled to his feet. "Now it's my turn," he said.

"Oh, forget it," said the farmer. "You can have the duck."

"The administration has been getting a lot of criticism for how they handled the situation. First, they didn't tell the media for almost a full day after it happened. The White House press corps was furious. They expect to be told when the vice president shoots a seventy-eight-year-old man in the face."

—Jimmy Kimmel

"How powerful a man do you have to be to shoot a man in the face and have that person say, 'My bad'?"

—Jon Stewart

bers duly chosen and sworn." In other words, you are most likely going to need sixty-seven votes on any of the charges. If that happens, the official is removed from office. But you may also hit the jackpot, because the Senate can also bar that person from holding any future public office. And, just because someone is convicted in the impeachment process doesn't exclude him or her from being brought up on criminal or civil proceedings for the same offense.

1 Last Thing to Worry About

According to the Constitution, the president must take an oath of office: "I do solemnly swear (or affirm) that I will faithfully execute the Office of President of the United States, and will to the best of my Ability, preserve protect and defend the Constitution of the United States."

There is no such oath for the vice president.

ACKNOWLEDGMENTS

I am deeply indebted to the many people who took time out from their busy lives to think about Dick Cheney. Although few of them have forgiven me, I'd like to thank them anyway: Michael Adams, Robert Anbian, Bob Asahina, David Auchincloss, Charles Austin, Suzie Bolotin, Jess Brallier, Brendan Burford, Nancy Butkus, Doug Chapin, Mark Davis, Tim Dobbins, Alan Emtage, Doug Hamilton, Jay Kennedy, Rick Kot, Heidi Krupp, John Marcom, Barbara Marcus, Kathy Matthews, Leslie Killip Mish, Mary Murphy, David Noonan, Richard Pine, Bobby Rhodes, Michael Rhodes, Kitty Ross, Tim Sanders, Glenn Sinclair, Rich Turner, and Bryant Wieneke.

The haiku experts deserve special mention: John Daschbach, John Lowell, Richard P. McDonough, and the haiku master of Shelbyville, Kentucky, John Scheidt.

A special thank you to Caroline Keith (of the Nyack, New York, store, C. Keith Vintage) and to the *Duck!* contributors: Rob Battles, Dennis Burke, Lisa Duchene, John Godges, Stephen Goldstone, John Hartmann, Joshua Hammer, Doris Haddock, Polly King, George Lattimore, Eugene Linden, Mark Liponis, Bruce McCall, Laurie Notaro, Carl Pritzkat, Harry Prichett, Terry Real, R. D. Rosen, Mitch Rustad, Miranda Spencer, Tony Travostino,

Lucian Truscott IV, Jen White, Francis Wilkinson, and the agent known as X.

The book owes its existence to the staff at Random House and their colleagues: the excellent editor Bruce Tracy and his associate Adam Korn, as well as Gina Centrello, Benjamin Dreyer, Barbara Fillon, Richard Elman, Lisa Feuer, Laura Goldin, Al Greco, Jonathan Jao, Jennifer Jones, Carole Lowenstein, Elizabeth McGuire, Beth Pearson, Maralee Youngs, Steven Meyers, Chris Furry, Thomas Perry, Beck Stvan, Jacqueline Updike, and my friend Don Weisberg.

ABOUT THE AUTHOR

GENE STONE is the author of the *New York Times* bestseller *The Bush Survival Bible*. A former newspaper, magazine, and book editor (as well as a former Peace Corps volunteer in Niger), he has collaborated on thirty books, written articles for numerous national magazines, and is a featured blogger on Huffingtonpost.com.